Praise for
Power and Purity

"Those seeking to understand the contemporary Social Justice Warrior phenomenon blighting the public square often turn to Karl Marx. But Mark T. Mitchell points us to another epochal nineteenth-century thinker: Friedrich Nietzsche, whose teachings are far more influential than many grasp. *Power and Purity* is a vital key unlocking the mysterious forces behind today's revolutionary challenges to a decaying democratic order. This book's brevity and its razor-sharp clarity make it accessible to both students and ordinary readers, who desperately need to grapple with the ideas that increasingly dominate our post-Christian peoples."
  —Rod Dreher, author of *The Benedict Option*

"Nearly everyone has a theory on the rise of identity politics and illiberalism on the left, but no one has seen further and more deeply than Mark Mitchell. Recognizing its root causes in the caustic wedding of Nietzsche's 'will to power' and a Puritanism without Christian grace, Mitchell weaves a compelling and frightening story of a new philosophy informing the intolerant tactics of the 'woke.' More frightening still, these currents arise from within currents of Western civilization itself, meaning that any remedy to this pathology requires a self-cure. Reading Mitchell's book is an indispensable first step."
  —Patrick Deneen, professor of political science at the University of Notre Dame and author of *Why Liberalism Failed*

"After several decades in which identity politics has grown ever stronger, we are converging on the true account of its causes and of the immense damage it is doing. Identity politics is the ghost of Christianity, stripped of its capacity to redeem and to renew. In the late nineteenth century, Nietzsche anticipated the rough outlines of this spiritual disease that would befall us. Drawing from Nietzsche's life and writings, Mark Mitchell's *Power and Purity* is the twenty-first-century guide we need to understand the spiritual disease of identity politics in full."

—Joshua Mitchell, professor of political theory at Georgetown University

"Why is it that postmodernists, who believe there are no moral absolutes, are so moralistic? Why have universities replaced rational discourse with silencing and punishing those who hold dissident ideas? Why is identity politics so vicious? Having read Mark Mitchell's *Power and Purity*, now I know. The seminal thinker for our day is Friedrich Nietzsche, who reduces all of culture, ideas, and life itself to the will to power. Mitchell unpacks both Nietzsche's influence and his predictions. And yet few people—for now—follow his moral nihilism, with even the hard left upholding values Nietzsche despised, such as equality and compassion. The Christian influence remains, even for those who believe with Nietzsche that God is dead. In fact, the left is employing a mash-up of Nietzsche and a secularized Puritanism, which has rejected God while cultivating self-righteousness and the zeal to censor, control, and punish. This book, which combines scholarly depth and a lively, readable style, will help readers navigate the strange paradoxes of contemporary politics, academia, and culture."

—Gene Edward Veith, provost and professor of literature emeritus at Patrick Henry College

POWER AND PURITY

Power
and Purity

The Unholy Marriage That Spawned
America's Social Justice Warriors

Mark T. Mitchell

REGNERY GATEWAY

Regnery Gateway™ is a trademark of Salem Communications Holding Corporation;
Regnery® is a registered trademark of Salem Communications Holding Corporation

ISBN 978-1-68451-011-5
ebook ISBN 978-1-68451-021-4

LCCN: 2019955287

Published in the United States by
Regnery Gateway, an imprint of
Regnery Publishing
A Division of Salem Media Group
300 New Jersey Ave NW
Washington, DC 20001
www.Regnery.com

Manufactured in the United States of America

10 9 8 7 6 5 4 3 2 1

Books are available in quantity for promotional or premium use. For information on discounts and terms, please visit our website: www.Regnery.com

To my students

Contents

INTRODUCTION
Nietzsche's Puritan Warriors   1

CHAPTER 1
My Truth, Your Truth, God and Values   19

CHAPTER 2
Protest Trumps Debate   31

CHAPTER 3
Democracy as Decadence   41

CHAPTER 4
Identity Politics: There Will Be Blood   49

CHAPTER 5
Memory, Monuments, and Manipulation   61

CHAPTER 6
OMG! The Weaponization of Language   71

CHAPTER 7
Life, Death, Sex, Babies, and Gender   83

CHAPTER 8
Creating the Overman: Technology and the
Promise of Unlimited Power   95

CHAPTER 9
"Higher" Education and the War on Reason   107

CHAPTER 10
Going Full Nietzsche: Do You Have the Guts?   119

CONCLUSION
In Search of a Saving Myth   131

Acknowledgments   139
Notes   141
Index   145

Books by Nietzsche Referred to in the Text

Unless otherwise indicated, citations to Nietzsche refer to section number rather than page number.

AC   *The Anti-Christ*, translated by H. L. Mencken (Tucson, Arizona: See Sharp Press, 1999).

BGE   *Beyond Good and Evil* in *Basic Writings of Nietzsche*, translated by Walter Kaufmann (New York: Modern Library, 1992).

BT   *The Birth of Tragedy* in *Basic Writings of Nietzsche*, translated by Walter Kaufmann (New York: Modern Library, 1992).

EH   *Ecce Homo* in *Basic Writings of Nietzsche*, translated by Walter Kaufmann (New York: Modern Library, 1992).

GS   *The Gay Science*, translated by Walter Kaufmann (New York: Vintage Books, 1974).

GM   *Genealogy of Morals* in *Basic Writings of Nietzsche*, translated by Walter Kaufmann (New York: Modern Library, 1992).

EI   *On the Future of Our Educational Institutions*, published as *Anti-Education: On the Future of Our Educational Institutions*, translated by Damion Searls (New York: New York Review of Books, 2016).

Z   *Thus Spoke Zarathustra*, translated by Walter Kaufmann (New York: Modern Library, 1995).

TI   *Twilight of the Idols*, translated by Richard Polt (Indianapolis: Hackett Publishing, 1997).

WP   *The Will to Power*, translated by Walter Kaufmann (New York: Vintage Books, 1968).

Nietzsche's Puritan Warriors

D uring the immigration debate in the summer of 2018, Congresswoman Maxine Waters of California told a crowd:

For these members of [President Trump's] Cabinet who remain and try to defend him, they're not going to be able to go to a restaurant, they're not going to be able to stop at a gas station, they're not going to be able to shop at a department store. The people are going to turn on them, they're going to protest, they're going to absolutely harass them.... If you see anybody from that Cabinet in a restaurant, in a department store, at a gasoline station, you get out and you create a crowd and you push back on them! And you tell them that they are not welcome, anymore, anywhere.[1]

In other words, a member of the U.S. Congress openly advocated the harassment of political opponents. While some tried to distance themselves from this rhetoric, others took up the cudgel. Both elected officials and high-profile staffers who dared to oppose the left were harassed in public places by hostile and threatening activists, who were absolutely convinced of the righteousness of their cause.

The contentious debate over Brett Kavanaugh's confirmation as a justice of the U.S. Supreme Court provoked similar expressions of fury on the left. Annie Shields of *The Nation* tweeted, "I'm starting a National @DemSocialists working group to follow [Senator] Jeff Flake around to every restaurant, Café, store, etc. he goes to for the rest of his life and yell at him." She followed up with, "If they knew they would get yelled at for the rest of their lives maybe they would act right."

Professor Christine Fair of Georgetown University's security studies program contributed her own incisive analysis with this tweet:

> Look at this chorus of entitled white men justifying a serial rapist's arrogated entitlement. All of them deserve miserable deaths while feminists laugh as they take their last gasps. Bonus: we castrate their corpses and feed them to swine? Yes.

Not to be outdone, the activist Alexis Grenell began a *New York Times* column titled "White Women, Come Get Your People"[2] with this sanguinary sentence:

> After a confirmation process where women all but slit their wrists, letting their stories of sexual trauma run like rivers of blood through the Capitol, the Senate still voted to confirm Judge Brett M. Kavanaugh to the Supreme Court.

She continued with a racially-charged condemnation of Judge Kavanaugh's supporters:

> These women are gender traitors. . . . We're talking about white women. The same 53 percent who put their racial privilege ahead of their second-class gender status in 2016 by voting to uphold a system that values only their whiteness, just as they have for decades.

Grenell's main target was white women who refused to jump on the "destroy Brett Kavanaugh" train. Aghast at the irrational evil of women who demanded corroborating evidence of sexual assault, she wrote:

The people who scare me the most are the mothers, sisters and wives of those young men, because my stupid uterus still holds out some insane hope of solidarity.

In case you missed it, Ms. Grenell and her hopeful uterus are angry. Very angry. Her ire was focused on Senator Susan Collins, who happens to be a woman (but is, alas, also white) and cast a crucial vote in favor of Kavanaugh's confirmation. Here's Grenell:

Meanwhile, Senator Collins subjected us to a slow funeral dirge about due process and some other nonsense I couldn't even hear through my rage headache as she announced on Friday she would vote to confirm Judge Kavanaugh. Her mostly male colleagues applauded her.

It should be noted that Ms. Grenell is herself a white woman, but she is clearly woke to the unfortunate realities of her identity.

What's going on? While no faction has a monopoly on extremism, a certain kind of behavior and rhetoric has become a hallmark of the left, especially among the so-called "elites," who fancy themselves the vanguard of the revolution against the straight, white patriarchy. Not convinced? Imagine a male professor's fantasizing aloud about the slow deaths of his female opponents, complete with the mutilation of their bodies. Does he keep his job? (He shouldn't.) Or imagine the *New York Times'* publishing an op-ed piece in favor of white nationalism or the subjugation of women or any other atrocious notion commonly attributed to everyone on the right. It is inconceivable. Although some on the right hold deplorable ideas, they are consigned to the fringes, while the radicals on the left enjoy positions of cultural and political influence.

The ascendancy of radicalism on the left is a threat to American society. All who believe that rational debate is the best means of identifying and achieving the common good—and this includes old-school liberals—must take this new radicalism seriously. These activists are willing to take extreme measures to achieve the paradise of justice and equality of which they dream.

◆

Something is clearly wrong. Americans are on edge. Political differences have hardened. Discourse has become crasser, positions more extreme. Political opponents are seen as enemies to be destroyed rather than fellow citizens and neighbors. Has it always been this way? To be sure, politics has always been a contact sport. Political differences have frequently provoked sharp words, occasionally accompanied by the wielding of sharp objects. But today our political differences have spilled over into daily life, spreading rancor and crowding out the common decencies that keep civil society civil. The American Dream, an image that has loomed large in the past, seems to be fading. The very definition of citizenship is being questioned. What does it mean to be an American? What binds us together? A common creed? A common history? A common religion or culture? None of these seems adequate today. And it goes without saying that mutual disdain is an inadequate binding agent.

Various thinkers have attempted to make sense of our condition. Some blame it on the 1960s—everything was fine until the Beatles showed up, Vietnam went down, and Woodstock got crazy. But that explanation is superficial. After all, if the 1960s brought about the decline of society, what brought about the 1960s? Ideas have antecedents as well as consequences. Perhaps the New Deal is the root of the problem. Or the despair and alienation precipitated by World War I. Or maybe we need to blame progressivism. Or the Industrial Revolution. Or slavery and the oppression of women. Perhaps the West was built on the systematic oppression of minorities by a white patriarchy that will release its hold on power only if compelled to do so.

Power may in fact lie at the heart of the story or at least be an indispensable feature of the tale. It was Friedrich Nietzsche—the great prophet of our age—who asserted that all of life is merely the will to power. If so, perhaps we should not be surprised that the patriarchy, if there is such a thing, asserts itself. Nor should we be surprised that the oppressed assert their own power by attempting to overthrow the oppressor and establish new ideals and a new power structure.

There is, of course, another way to reckon with the facts. Perhaps the West in general, and America in particular, has lost the courage of its convictions. No society can long survive if it no longer believes it deserves to survive. Could it be that the greatness of the West is rooted in a commitment to truths now deemed untenable by many? I use the term "greatness" realizing that many will scoff, but their scoffing only demonstrates what I am asserting: We have lost faith in the very ideals that made us who we were. We are attacking our roots. But if the branches attack the roots, the tree will be devastated. Branches, despite their noble intentions and self-righteousness, do not fare well in such an enterprise.

What ideals formed America? What notions have shaped the way Americans think about the world and themselves? Alexis de Tocqueville noted that if you want to understand a nation, you need to consider its infancy, its formative moment: "Peoples always feel [the effects] of their origins. The circumstances that accompanied their birth and served to develop them influence the entire course of the rest of their lives."[3] And America, according to Tocqueville, is at its heart a Puritan nation. Even though most of us have long ago abandoned any conscious affiliation with Puritanism—and perhaps vehemently deny any sympathy with it—we have inherited habits, ideas, and institutions deeply influenced by our Puritan past.

To put it more broadly, America continues to be profoundly shaped by its Christian heritage. Even those who most emphatically reject any allegiance to Christianity remain deeply implicated. The language of rights and the ideals of equality and democracy that pervade our political discourse are unimaginable apart from Christianity. Nietzsche understood this, and he was deeply dismayed by the nearly indelible fingerprints of Christianity on the Western consciousness.

There is a dramatic difference between a pre-Christian society and a post-Christian one. Pre-Christian pagan societies look radically different from societies formed by a prolonged encounter with Christianity. It is not easy to shake off the lingering effects of a Christian past. The residue is nearly impossible to eradicate. Although citizens may deny the faith, ignore the churches, and make every effort to ignore the social and moral teachings of the church, the fact remains that we live in a Christ-haunted culture. Our institutions, our language, our habits, the very shape of our consciousness, are Christian. Even in denying the faith, Americans in many respects see the world through Christian eyes.

Puritanism, of course, has become a term of disparagement, in part because of an increasing suspicion of Christianity and in part because of a distorted view of Puritanism going back at least to the fiction of Nathaniel Hawthorne. Puritans had a keen sense of human sinfulness and were deeply concerned with fostering social and political institutions that encouraged virtue and discouraged vice. They sought personal holiness made possible by God's unmerited grace and a life of spiritual discipline. As fidelity to orthodox Christianity has waned, however, concepts such as sin and holiness have become distorted. Our culture retains a profound sense of sin, but secular progressivism limits it to a strong awareness of the sins of *others*—especially the perceived sins of institutions and social structures—losing the sense of original sin that infects every human being. Purity, therefore, can be attained or restored if compromised institutions and the persons complicit in those institutions are cleansed or, if necessary, eradicated. Holiness becomes a purely human endeavor. There is no need for divine grace, so there is no need for Christ. Divine redemption is replaced by human effort, forgiveness of sins by a purely human demand for punishment that the righteous can mete out on those who sin against the new secular but thoroughly moralistic order.

In this book I will argue that the unrest and sense of impending crisis we all feel are the result of a strange fusion of two seemingly incompatible ideas. Today's social justice warriors of the radical left embody a toxic combination of the Nietzschean will to power and Puritan moralism, secularized but no less rigorous than its earlier religious instantiation. Some will be inclined to dismiss this account as a typically academic effort to blame social and political problems on the musings (and often mutterings) of obscure thinkers few have read and even fewer have understood. Fair enough. But bear with me. *Ideas* matter. *Ideals* matter. We are all moved by our deepest beliefs, even if we haven't taken the time to articulate them—indeed, even if we don't recognize them. Consider, for example, the ideal of diversity. Most people today take it for granted that diversity is good, more diversity is better, and anything that thwarts the expansion of diversity is evil. This is an axiom of our age. But is it true? Even asking the question smacks of heresy, and indeed it is a heresy against the reigning orthodoxy.

But hold on, you might say, words like "heresy" and "orthodoxy" are religious terms. We dispensed with that outdated mode of thinking long ago when we disavowed our embarrassing Puritan past. Did we? Perhaps the story is more complicated than that. Perhaps we have abjured fidelity to ancient religious beliefs only to commit ourselves with equal ardor to a new faith, a new set of ideals, a new orthodoxy. Like those religious enthusiasts of old, our cultural leaders know that heretics are dangerous and that orthodoxy must be guarded by the faithful.

At the same time, how are we influenced by Nietzsche? Most Americans have not read him and might not even know how to pronounce his name, let alone spell it. Is this an indication of the failure of his ideas? Not necessarily. I want to suggest that Nietzsche's ideas have so permeated our world that we generally don't even notice them. A victorious ideology is as invisible as it is ubiquitous. It loses its aura of novelty and becomes the furniture of our minds. Some of Nietzsche's basic ideas have become just that. And they have been combined with certain Christian ingredients with one notable omission—Christ.

Of course, I have admittedly overstated the case in an important way. Not everyone has bought in to the reigning orthodoxy. There are still some on the outside who resist what many think is inevitable, who pit themselves against "the logic of history," as the enthusiasts like to put it. But even these holdouts have at times adopted the strategy and rhetoric of their opponents, not out of calculation ("If you can't beat 'em, join 'em") but because Nietzsche's thought has permeated virtually every quarter of our culture. Even those who think they oppose the radical ideology of the left too often find themselves embracing at least some of its tactics, terminology, and assumptions. This should comfort the partisans of this brave new ideology, for when your opponents have adopted your underlying assumptions, victory is all but guaranteed.

This book attempts to make sense of our current malaise, especially the impulses driving identity politics and the social justice warriors of the radical left. For Nietzsche, life is nothing but the will to power: the attempt to assert oneself against others who are motivated by the same headlong drive. The Puritan is motivated by a quest for moral and political purity. By analyzing this odd combination, we can understand what is at stake and how to respond.

◆

First, however, it might be helpful to take a brief look at Nietzsche's life. It is tempting to say that, above all else, he was a lonely man. Friedrich Nietzsche was born in 1844 in Röcken, Germany. He described his father, a Lutheran pastor, as "the perfect picture of a country parson! Endowed with a good spirit and heart, adorned with all the virtues of a Christian, he led a quiet and simple but happy life."[4] Years later, Nietzsche wrote, "I consider it a great privilege to have had a father like this: it even seems to me that this explains any other privileges I might have—even apart from life."[5] Nietzsche was five years old when his father died. Six months later, his two-year-old brother died. The family, reduced to Friedrich, his mother, his younger sister, and two unmarried aunts, left Röcken and settled in Naumburg, living on savings and a modest pension.

Nietzsche was a sensitive and studious child. His fellow students called him "the little pastor" because, as his sister later wrote, he could recite "biblical verses and spiritual songs" with such emotion that "you almost had to cry." At the age of twelve he wrote his first philosophical essay, "On the Origin of Evil." He loved music, became proficient at the piano, and filled notebooks with his poetry. Nevertheless, he was aware of a profound absence. "By and large, I am in charge of my own upbringing.... I have had to do without the strict and senior guidance of a male intellect."[6]

A brilliant student, Nietzsche was awarded a place in an elite boarding school, where he received a superb education in the classics. He enrolled at the University of Bonn, intending to study theology, but his interests soon turned decisively toward philology—the study of language.

In 1865, while visiting Cologne, he asked a porter to take him to a restaurant. As a joke, the porter instead took him to a brothel. Nietzsche later recalled, "I found myself suddenly surrounded by half a dozen apparitions in tinsel and gauze, looking at me expectantly. For a short space of time I was speechless." Nietzsche touched nothing but the piano, an indication of the powerful pull music had on him. "I made instinctively for the piano as being the only soulful thing present. I struck a few chords, which freed me from my paralysis, and I escaped."[7] Some, including the novelist Thomas Mann, speculate that he later returned and touched more than the piano, in the process contracting syphilis. The evidence that he returned is inconclusive, however, and scholars debate whether he suffered from syphilis.

When he returned home for the Easter holidays in 1865, Nietzsche caused his mother much grief by expressing an unwillingness to attend church, and he refused to take communion on Easter Sunday. Nietzsche's younger sister, Elisabeth, who admired her brother almost to the point of worship, was powerfully influenced by his wavering faith. She sought out pastoral counsel but found it unsatisfying.[8]

Nietzsche spent a year in military service, during which he was injured in a riding accident. Continuing his studies, he so impressed his professors that he was recommended for a professorial position at the University of Basel even before he completed his dissertation. A tireless worker, energetic teacher, and prolific writer, he was nevertheless physically weak. Declining health forced him to resign from the university in 1879. He was granted a small pension that afforded some independence but few luxuries. A biographer provides a vivid description of Nietzsche's life after the university:

> He is shy, about five-foot-eight, but a little stooped, almost blind, reserved, unaffected, and especially polite; he lives in modest boarding houses in Sils Maria, Nizza, Mentone, Rome, Turin. This is how Stefan Zweig brings him to life for us: "Carefully the myopic man sits down to a table; carefully, the man with the sensitive stomach considers every item on the menu: whether the tea is not too strong, the food

not spiced too much, for every mistake in his diet upsets his sensitive digestion, and every transgression in his nourishment wreaks havoc with his quivering nerves for days. No glass of wine, no glass of beer, no alcohol, no coffee at his place, no cigar and no cigarette after his meal, nothing that stimulates, refreshes, or rests him: only the short meager meal and a little urbane, unprofound conversation in a soft voice with an occasional neighbor (as a man speaks who for years has been unused to talking and is afraid of being asked too much).

"And up again into the small, narrow, modest, coldly furnished *chambre garnie*, where innumerable notes, pages, writings, and proofs are piled up on the table, but no flower, no decoration, scarcely a book and rarely a letter. Back in a corner, a heavy and graceless wooden trunk, his only possession, with the two shirts and the other worn suit. Otherwise only books and manuscripts, and on a tray innumerable bottles and jars and potions: against the migraines, which often render him all but senseless for hours, against his stomach cramps, against spasmodic vomiting, against the slothful intestines, and above all the dreadful sedatives against his insomnia, chloral hydrate and Veronal. A frightful arsenal of poisons and drugs, yet the only helpers in the empty silence of this strange room in which he never rests except in brief and artificially conquered sleep. Wrapped in his overcoat and a woolen scarf (for the wretched stove smokes only and does not give warmth), his fingers freezing, his double glasses pressed close to the paper, his hurried hand writes for hours—words the dim eyes can hardly decipher. For hours he sits like this and writes until his eyes burn."[9]

For ten years after his resignation, Nietzsche wandered Europe, ill and ill at ease, yet producing a steady stream of books, notable for their provocative arguments and an energetic and idiosyncratic style. Titles include *Beyond Good and Evil*, *The Genealogy of Morals*, *The Twilight of the Idols*, and *The Anti-Christ*.

Perhaps it is little wonder that a man who declared that all of life is the will to power found his greatest satisfaction and delight in improvising on the piano. The freedom, creativity, and power of the artist is a theme running throughout Nietzsche's work. This is not limited to the creation of art, as such, for the artistic impulse governs all who are powerful, including those who command: "Their work is an instinctive creation and imposition of forms; they are the most involuntary, unconscious artists there are—wherever they appear something new soon arises.... [T]hey appear as lightning appears, too terrible, too sudden, too convincing, too 'different' even to be hated" (GM, II, 17). Lightning, creativity, power, freedom—these go together. Once after hiking near Leipzig, he described a storm: "How different the lightning, the storm, the hail, free powers, without ethics! How happy, how powerful they are, pure will, untarnished by intellect!"[10] When he describes the Overman, Nietzsche employs the image of lightning: "Behold, I teach you the overman: he is this lightning, he is this frenzy" (Z, prologue, 3).

At times, Nietzsche's work seemed to produce adverse effects in his own psyche: "My doctrine that the world of good and evil is only an apparent and perspectivist world is such an innovation that sometimes I lose my ability to hear or see."[11] He proposed to two women, both of whom declined. He repeatedly wrote of his solitude, noting in 1888 that "I have gradually broken off almost all contact with other people, out of disgust that they take me to be something other than I am."[12] In the same year, he wrote, "The fact is 'that I am so sad'; the problem 'I don't know what that means.'"[13]

In 1889, Nietzsche collapsed in the streets of Turin. He never recovered. He spent the next decade in the care of others, physically ill and mentally insane. He died in 1900 unaware of his growing fame and the spreading influence of his writing.

What follows is an exploration of a curious union of Nietzschean thought and Puritan moralism in our central cultural institutions and practices. As we go, it will become increasingly evident that the ideas of Nietzsche have touched, and in some instances completely transformed, certain aspects of our society. Furthermore, we shall see how those ideas have been incoherently combined with Puritan moralism to produce in their adherents a self-righteous conviction of their own moral purity. This unholy marriage of power and purity has given birth to the social justice movement led by a peculiar breed that we might call Nietzsche's Puritan Warriors.

CHAPTER 1

My Truth, Your Truth, God and Values

Today people often refer to truth as if it were a personal possession. "That's my truth," someone might say. Or, "That's your truth, but it's just not true for me." This is a curious way of speaking if truth is, well, *true*.

It was once believed that the world existed in a certain way, that men could know something about that world, and that to know correctly was to know what was true. Gravity, for instance, is real. If you jump from a high building, you will learn some hard truths about the world. Or at least one. The world was once thought to contain moral truths as well, which were ignored only at our peril. To murder is wrong, and such an act merits moral guilt and deserves punishment. Likewise lying, stealing, and sassing your parents. Truth, in this older sense, was understood as a feature of reality, and our minds were capable of grasping, albeit imperfectly, various aspects of that reality.

Something, however, has changed. How did we get to a point where "truth" is spoken of as nothing more than a personal preference—akin, say, to liking chocolate ice cream more than vanilla? That's my truth. Vanilla might be your truth, and if so, that's fine. We're cool. We're just different. Of course, it's much easier to play this game with "abstract" moral categories than with physical reality. If you don't subscribe to "my truth" about the perils of stepping in front of a moving bus, the disadvantages of "your truth" may eventually make themselves tragically felt.

We must admit up front, though, that plenty of life choices are, in fact, rooted in personal preferences. I may order steak, while you order kale. I may become a teacher, and you go to medical school. In both cases, our differing preferences are obvious, but it is not readily apparent that either choice is morally better. Many choices we make are like this, for in a world of alternatives, we are often confronted with more than one good option.

But there are limits. While I can choose to be a teacher or a doctor, I cannot choose to be a squirrel. I cannot choose to be an Eskimo or a woman. "But wait," someone might object, "there are people who identify as creatures other than human—they call themselves 'otherkin.'" And some men declare themselves women (and vice versa), and any number of physicians will obligingly prescribe hormones and snip away the "inconvenient truth" in an effort to deny what in an earlier age was regarded as obvious. Still, our power to choose extends only so far. At the genetic level, there is no such thing as transgender.[1] And the NAACP of Spokane refused to pretend that its one-time president Rachel Dolezal, a white woman, was black, however intensely she "identified" as such.

◆

What has all this to do with Nietzsche? Plenty. And it is necessary to grasp the scope and audacity of Nietzsche's project to understand how pertinent he is today—both as a prophet of our time and as a critic of our society.

Nietzsche famously, or perhaps infamously, declared the death of God. Of course, he did not mean that literally. He was not suggesting that God ate a bad date, got sick, and keeled over. Nor was he saying that God died of old age, although that is closer to what he meant. Nietzsche meant that the *idea* of God was no longer plausible. But he was not content simply to drop his bombshell and walk away. Nietzsche was concerned with the aftermath. He understood better than most that the "death" of God would reverberate throughout Western culture. Philosophy, morality, politics, history, language, religious practice, psychology—nothing was immune, and everything would have to be rebuilt from the ground up.

What Nietzsche grasped, as many of his more timid contemporaries did not, was that men could not cease to believe in God and continue living as if nothing had changed. For instance, you cannot declare the death of God and continue to assert traditional moral categories, insisting that people observe the Golden Rule or some similar principle of benevolence or fellow feeling. As Nietzsche so provocatively put it, the value of values must be reconsidered. He sought to get "beyond good and evil" (the title of one of his books), for good and evil are rooted in assumptions about the nature of reality. Concepts like guilt, shame, and resentment are merely the hoary remnants of an obsolete system.

Before Nietzsche, moral philosophers had hotly debated the rational justification for moral duties. Some based their claims on divine commands, some on natural law, others more recently on rationality itself or the so-called "greatest happiness" principle. Nietzsche wanted to get at something more fundamental. Rather than bicker about how to rationally justify basic moral principles that everyone agrees on—don't murder, don't steal, tell the truth, and so forth—Nietzsche asked a more disquieting question: Why affirm these age-old values at all? Perhaps they have been fabricated over time by those seeking to assert their own wills over others. Perhaps the language of the "common good" and "love thy neighbor" are merely ways to neuter the powerful by getting them to voluntarily suppress their desires so they don't break out against the weak and timid. Perhaps the categories of good and evil represent the greatest fraud in history, a fraud made possible by the now defunct belief in an all-powerful deity who could coerce us to do his will with the threat of eternal punishment in the next life and a persistent sense of guilt in this one.

Greek philosophers such as Plato and Aristotle, along with Christian thinkers who came later, held that the cosmos was a morally configured reality and that human beings could flourish only if their lives conformed to reality. To act justly meant to act in a way that corresponded to a reality that was "outside" of the self, a reality that existed prior to human will. The will, therefore, was subordinate to (or obliged by) a reality it did not create. Nature or God preceded human will, and to act contrary to nature or God was to condemn oneself to frustration and unhappiness. Flourishing, happiness, and health were inextricably tied to a willing submission to knowable standards not devised by human will. Without God, however, the cosmos has no intrinsic moral structure. There are no moral conditions for happiness or flourishing, only a chaotic array of individuals and natural systems that "happened." Submission to a "higher" power or to an "outside" moral standard, then, is an unreasonable concession to an imaginary "reality," something akin to submitting to the purple unicorn in the sky—a charming game for children, perhaps, but something of an embarrassment for adults.

What about the notion of truth itself? To answer that question, we need to go back to the fourth century B.C. Plato, according to Nietzsche, is responsible for establishing "truth" as the West's highest ideal. He argued that there exists a realm of "pure spirit," a reality beyond the merely physical and of which the physical is at best a dim reflection. A feature of this realm of pure spirit, taught Plato, is "the good," a reality "beyond being" that gives life and meaning to all that exists. For Plato, the *most real* is also the *most good*. When a man dies, his soul, freed from its physical prison, becomes fully what it is capable of becoming. Nietzsche declared that "Christianity is Platonism for 'the people'" (BGE, Preface). His criticisms of Platonism, therefore, apply equally to Christianity. Both, he charged, despise the body and this world. Both posit a perfect Good to which men ought to submit. And both find solace in a world of spirit that transcends bodily existence and even temporality itself.

Nietzsche believed that the illusory Platonic and Christian construct was breaking down, allowing people to begin "breathing freely again." In his view, God and truth go hand in hand, and on this point he agreed with Plato and the Christians. The Greeks and later the Christians thought of truth as somehow participating in the divine. Heraclitus of Ephesus (d. 475 B.C.) posited that all things come to be in accordance with the "logos," which for him was a general principle by which the world is governed. He identified it with fire. When Saint John called Christ the *logos*, he was appropriating this image and explicitly identifying Christ with the divine. *Logos* means "word," but it also can mean "rational principle," suggesting that Christ represents a sort of divine order that can be articulated through language.

If truth exists, and if it is inextricably tied to theism, then a commitment to the notion of truth must entail a commitment to theism. We will be "under the thumb" of a divine will, obliged to submit to a cosmos ordered and superintended by God. To be committed to the idea of truth, then, is to be bound, limited, and constrained. To be "free spirits"—a term Nietzsche used regularly—we must extricate ourselves from that increasingly far-fetched notion of God. It is here, Nietzsche believed, that twenty centuries of "training in truthfulness" will actually turn the tables on theism, for belief in God has become a problem, and those committed to the idea of truth will be forced to face the problem head on. They will have to recognize that God is, in fact, dead. At this point, however, their commitment to truth will turn on itself with a vengeance, for once God is jettisoned, the very notion of truth must be called into question. No longer will we speak of truth, dragging along with it the musty implication of theism. Now we can see more clearly that life is not the will to truth but the will to power. Faith in God is replaced with faith in man, and the will to truth is replaced by the will to power.

It is important to recognize that Christianity was Nietzsche's central target. All of his work can be understood as an attempt to destroy the faith of his father. The psychology of his vendetta would be an interesting study,[2] but for now we need to focus on his arguments. In perhaps the most famous of all his declarations of God's death—his parable *The Madman*—Nietzsche presents a Diogenes-like character who lights a lantern, runs to the marketplace, and declares to the astonished onlookers that God is dead. He goes further. God is dead, and "we have killed him."

Like Nietzsche, this madman realizes that one cannot kill God and continue on as if nothing had changed. Acknowledging the enormous consequences of this news and the stunning hubris necessary to bring it to light, Nietzsche asks, "Who gave us the sponge to wipe away the entire horizon? What were we doing when we unchained this earth from its sun?" Both images suggest a loss of orientation. Wiping away the horizon makes traditional navigation—using a sextant fixed on a star and the horizon—impossible. When the earth is unchained from the sun, the days and seasons cannot be marked. Where will we go? How can we navigate? Are there no fixed stars? No fixed morality? No heaven? No hell? No justice? No good? No evil? How can we bear this new world free from the shackles of God? How can we reorient ourselves to this new reality? "What festivals of atonement, what sacred games shall we have to invent? Is not the greatness of this deed too great for us? Must we ourselves not become gods simply to appear worthy of it?" (GS, 125).

Yet hope remains. Perhaps not for the weak, who find comfort and security in the cocoon of theistic belief. But for the strong and free spirits, this turn of events represents "a new dawn" with new possibilities. Nevertheless, Nietzsche understood that the full implications of the death of God would take time to reveal themselves and to make their way down to the very marrow of Western society, steeped so long in Christianity.

Nietzsche especially despised nineteenth-century moral philosophers, both Kantians and utilitarians, who sought to preserve the basic outlines of traditional morality—don't murder, don't lie, don't steal, seek justice, and so forth—but at the same time eliminated the concept of God or divine law from their respective ethical frameworks. Nietzsche recognized more clearly than most that if we rid the world of God we also dispense with Christian morality—that is to say, European morality. The two stand or fall together.

If Nietzsche was right about that, what becomes of traditional morality? If there are "no moral facts," (TI, p. 38) then how do we account for the ubiquity and power of moral claims and demands? To answer this obvious question, Nietzsche embarked on his "genealogical" project, presenting a purely naturalistic account of the development of morality. As we saw, Nietzsche thought the will to truth must ultimately be subsumed into the will to power. Likewise, the will to morality must be understood in light of this more fundamental urge.

A philologist, Nietzsche began by uncovering what might be called the primordial significance of basic moral terms. Initially, "good" referred not to a moral category but to a state of health, strength, and vitality, associated with what he called the "knightly-aristocratic" class. "Bad," not surprisingly, was merely the opposite, associated with a plebian or common social class. The category of "evil" did not exist. It had to be invented. But who would come up with such a notion? What could be their motive? The answer is obvious if we are willing to follow Nietzsche. The weak invented "evil," and their motive was the will to power, which is at the heart of all motives. Not content to wallow in their weakness, they sought to reverse their fortunes and by an act of philosophical jujitsu gain power over the powerful. This they achieved by what Nietzsche called "the transvaluation of values," an account we can admire at least for its creativity.

The knightly-aristocratic class was confronted by the "priestly" class, which, lacking physical vitality, sought subversive ways to assert its power. The priests invented the notion of guilt and insisted that qualities that had hitherto been seen as good—power, strength, nobility, wealth—were "evil." Good became identified with the very qualities that were once seen as bad: weakness, poverty, suffering, and so forth. This transvaluation of values is clearly seen in the teachings of Jesus: blessed are the meek, the poor, the suffering, the persecuted. The very qualities Nietzsche called bad and which are clearly undesirable from a particular vantage point, Christ associated with blessing.

Of course, Jesus was a Jew, a member of the "priestly people" that had for centuries been oppressed by the strong and had in those years built up a profound resentment against its oppressors. This priestly people did the unthinkable: it discovered a way to triumph over its adversaries, not by force but by audacious cleverness, devising a means by which its masters would willingly submit to its dark and unnatural desires. How? By rejecting Jesus and crucifying him, the Jews set the stage for the Roman conversion to Christianity. The triumph of this religion of the priestly class and of the weak, born of resentment, gave the West its moral categories and demands along with a profound sense of guilt that could be alleviated only by the ministrations of the church, the institution of priests that promises forgiveness through the body and blood of a crucified God.

The victory of Christianity produced the victory of the slaves and priests—both painfully impotent—who through malevolent treachery convinced the powerful to submit to the ideals of Christianity. Perhaps they weren't as impotent as they appeared.

Nietzsche saw Christianity and Christian morality as the mortal enemies of life itself. The weak have invented such concepts as God, the soul, truth, salvation, and free will, each of which undermines health and strength (EH, 789–90). As he put it, "Dionysus versus the 'Crucified': there you have the antithesis" (WP, 1052). The former represents life, vitality, destruction, and creation. The latter represents an innocent suffering to achieve salvation in another world. One is of this world. The other is not. One is healthy and strong and can tolerate suffering for the sake of greatness. The other is sick and weak and suffers at the hands of the strong.

For centuries, the priestly class—the Jews and therefore the Christians—found a way to exercise its will to power and thereby subjugate the powerful under the guise of guilt and the promise of redemption. Guilty men could be restored to a right relationship with God through the intercession of the church. With the ascendency of Christianity, the transvaluation of values was complete. By the nineteenth century, however, belief in God had begun to falter. The facade of Christian morality began to crumble. When Nietzsche made so bold as to declare the death of God, he was giving voice to a belief that had become increasingly common. Nietzsche, however, did something that his contemporaries were unwilling to do: He argued that the death of God forces a reconsideration of virtually all categories of life, including, as we have seen, morality and even truth itself. If there is no God, everything must change.

CHAPTER 2

Protest Trumps Debate

Intimidation works. We see this in the corporate world when employees are pressed to conform to standards of "progress" and "tolerance" and when political agendas are imposed on a city or state with the threat that a corporation will withdraw its business from that community if a certain law is not passed or rescinded. The same pressures abound in the academy, where the vast majority of professors call themselves liberal, but serious engagement with people holding substantially different viewpoints is increasingly rare. If a speaker's views do not line up with the current orthodoxy, he or she is shunned, shouted down, or driven away. The same tactics are common in the political arena. Consider the following examples.

In the spring of 2017, Charles Murray, a scholar at the American Enterprise Institute, attempted to give a lecture at Middlebury College in Vermont. The event was shut down by a mob—mostly students of that august liberal arts institution—whose disorderly protest sent a professor to the hospital.[1] Similar mob censorship is taking place at elite and not so elite universities around the country.

In July 2017, James Damore, a Google engineer, used his company's internal discussion board to argue that Google's culture had become an "echo chamber," that dissent from what Damore considered a liberal bias was not allowed, and that the disparity in the numbers of male and female programmers might reflect a difference of interests. Damore was accused of fomenting a hostile work environment and was fired.[2]

In June 2018, a group of protesters accosted the attorney general of Florida, Pam Bondi, outside a Tampa cinema, questioning her about health care policy and immigration. A video of the confrontation showed several people shouting at her as she left the theater, escorted by law enforcement officers. Fittingly enough, she had just watched a documentary called *Won't You Be My Neighbor?* about public television's Fred Rogers. Mr. Rogers would not be pleased.

Again in 2018, during a contentious "debate" about immigration policies, the secretary of the Department of Homeland Security, Kirstjen Nielsen, eating dinner in a D.C. restaurant, was surrounded by protestors shouting their disagreement about the administration's policies. She was forced to leave. Protestors also positioned themselves in front of her house, pacing with placards and angrily shouting their demands.

During the same immigration "debate," the White House press secretary, Sarah Huckabee Sanders, went to a restaurant in Lexington, Virginia. After her party was seated and had placed their orders, the owner asked them to leave, citing her strong disagreement with President Trump's policies.

A few days later, Congresswoman Maxine Waters delivered her infamous exhortation to harass members of the Trump administration at restaurants, department stores, and filling stations. To their credit, the Democratic congressional leaders—Senator Charles Schumer and Congresswoman Nancy Pelosi—condemned Waters's remarks, but activists on the left have followed her advice, driving their political opponents from public places as punishment for their heresies.

Maxine Waters did not invent this tactic. President Obama, on the stump in 2008, urged his supporters to confront their "friends and neighbors." Standing behind a sign promising "Change," he instructed his supporters: "I want you to argue with them, and get in their face"—the sort of advice you'd expect from someone who cut his teeth organizing communities based on the principles in Saul Alinsky's *Rules for Radicals*. However such tactics are framed, they amount to the intentional and systematic harassment of one's opponents.

The far right, of course, has its share of persons who are willing to resort to violence or the threat thereof, including the white nationalists who marched in Charlottesville, Virginia, in August 2017. One of them drove his car into a crowd of counter-protesters, killing a woman. The difference is that left-wing radicals have the sympathy of many cultural elites, while white nationalists are despised, finding no sympathy in the press or academia. This asymmetry can provoke a radicalized and embittered reaction. Right-minded Americans should reject radicals on both the left and the right, but until that happens, the impulse to violence will grow as political differences become more acute.

As politics gives way to protest, protest can escalate from the merely verbal to the physical. Rhetoric matters, and when groups persistently refer to their political opponents as enemies, a few will take such rhetoric literally. Once the shootings, the beatings, and the bombings begin, they are difficult to stop. In fact, in June 2018, a Rasmussen Report indicated that 31 percent of Americans believed a civil war was likely in the next five years.[3]

Our country is increasingly beset by protests and the threat of violence. The language of a common good—of moral ends that are proper to human beings, of a transcendent source of morality, or even of the existence of God—is threatened by the feverish demands for autonomy, liberation, rights, benefits, or whatever happens to be the demand of the moment.

We are at a crossroads. As tensions grow and animosity intensifies along with the rhetoric of warfare and destruction, it is not hard to imagine an incident—perhaps some confrontation between white nationalists and Antifa—that will spark general violence. On the other hand, it may be possible for responsible citizens to dial back the rhetoric, to speak respectfully to and about each other, and thus regain some sense of what joins us together as citizens. The stakes couldn't be higher.

◆

Not long ago, social conservatives were wringing their hands over the "moral relativism" of the young. Today, moral relativism is not the problem. Maybe it never was. If you listen to the rhetoric of the social justice warriors, you hear not the easygoing platitudes of the relativist but the hard-edged assertions of the absolutist. When people march in the streets, picket their opponent's house, and threaten their political enemies with violence, they are expressing not moral relativism but supreme moral confidence. The humility required to listen patiently and respond charitably has nearly vanished. We see in all of this the strange combination of moral absolutism, inherited from our Puritan past, and the Nietzschean will to power.

If power lies at the heart of all human affairs, then any appeal to reason to justify one's position is merely a means of leveraging power. For Nietzsche, right and wrong, and even true and false, are rooted in a theistic order that has died. Rationality is not a means by which men can determine truth or pursue a common good derived from human nature but

merely a means by which the will of the powerful can dominate the weak or the weak can seize power from the strong.

This turn has conspicuous implications for politics. The
classical ideal of politics—which the American founders
shared—is predicated on a moral order that is knowable, however imperfectly. Politics, according to this ideal, entails rational debate about the best means to secure ends proper to
human beings individually and corporately. It is an ongoing
discussion about the common good, and while that discussion
may veer from rational debate into hostility and force, the
ideal remains a clear indictment of the violent alternative.

In a world infused with Nietzschean assumptions, the
understanding of politics as a rational discussion about the
best means to secure ends rooted in the natural order has to
be abandoned. If there is no "good" independent of human
will; if there is no human nature that implies norms of behavior; if there is no God who created the cosmos and infused
human nature with meaning, purpose, and direction; if the
category of truth must be discarded, then "rational" discussion about those things is nothing more than the babbling of
men either deceived into imagining a world infused with
moral meaning or slyly employing the language of morality
to assert their will to power.

In a Nietzschean world, politics, at least in the classical sense,
is exchanged for alternative modes of discourse and persuasion.
Political protest marked by aggression, noise, and intimidation

replaces rational debate, for protest is the concentration of power in pursuit of the desires of individuals and groups. People are not persuaded by protests. They are drowned out.

Residual Puritanism is also apparent in the politics of protest. The salient feature of the activists and protestors in America today—especially among the social justice warriors of the radical left—is the moral absolutism behind their rhetoric and their actions. They use terms such as "rights," "equality," "democracy," and "tolerance" with confidence, absolutely certain that those who stand in the way of these noble ideals are racists, homophobes, fascists, or just plain evil. Following Nietzsche in their will to power, they are beholden to their Puritan ancestors (whom they despise for their religious bigotry) for their unshakeable sense of rectitude.

This new moral absolutism is irrational and indicates that the will to truth has been replaced by the will to power. The death of God necessarily entailed the death of truth. The new absolutism of our cultural moment is grounded in will rather than reason, and laments over the decline of rational debate are, in reality, an expression of longing for a theistic metaphysics that has been abandoned implicitly if not explicitly.

This new form of irrational moral absolutism is accompanied by a form of political absolutism that can be traced to a decline in the historical Christian distinction between politics and heavenly things. In the fifth century, Augustine argued that the City of God must be distinguished from the Earthly City and that while all men find themselves, for a time, part of the Earthly City, it is not of ultimate consequence. Politics is not to be neglected, for it is a means of attaining peace and justice, however imperfectly and impermanently. But it is secondary to the soul's eternal destiny. This view of politics avoids political fanaticism while providing space in which a chastened politics can operate. Since true happiness and perfect justice are achievable only in heaven, well beyond human influence, human beings must be content with incremental and reversible achievements in the Earthly City. Hope is deferred to heaven, and the imperfections and limitations of the earthly realm are patiently endured.

If God is dead, or at least no longer a central figure in political reflections, the "two-city" solution collapses. Dreams of political perfection, once deferred to the heavenly kingdom, are reintroduced in the temporal realm. The longing for perfection—born of a Christian notion of heaven—is difficult to forget. The chastened politics of the Christian era has been replaced by a revolutionary politics that seeks perfect justice and moral purity by political means. The French Revolution was the first of the revolutions springing from political perfectionism (the residue of a Christian heritage) and impatience with the slow pace of traditional political processes.

Revolution represents an alternative to politics and a complement to protest, for revolution seeks to accomplish immediately what the political process can achieve only gradually. Revolutionaries are always in a hurry. They lack the patience rooted in humility and a recognition that the human condition will never be radically altered by political means. Revolutionaries chant, "What do we want? Justice! When do we want it? Now!" But now is never soon enough, and justice or equality or whatever ideal the revolutionary is fixated on is never fully realized. So the revolutionary is never satisfied, and his methods become increasingly radical as his goal proves illusive.

Although many people—especially the social justice warriors—relish the idea of revolution, we would do well to consider the consequences, for revolutions rarely turn out well.[4] The rhetoric of revolution and war fosters the centralization of political power. War itself is perhaps the most efficient means of centralizing political power. Resistance to a threat, external or internal, requires the consolidation of authority and resources. The rhetoric of war tends to the same ends, and it is interesting to consider the extent to which the language of war has infected our political discourse. We have in recent decades declared war on poverty, drugs, illiteracy, and crime. Politicians wage "campaigns" and establish "war rooms" where they formulate strategies to defeat the "enemy."

When citizens come to think of politics in terms of war, they are drawn to violence rather than debate, absolutism rather than compromise, and they become willing to cede power to those who position themselves as best equipped to defeat the enemy. It is not hard to see how the pervasive use of war rhetoric—and therefore the rhetoric of power—eventually leads to violence and the breakdown of social cohesion. Social instability as a consequence of war rhetoric and revolutionary actions leads, if history is any indication, to an authoritarian backlash. Napoleon and Stalin were the unintended, though not surprising, consequences of revolutions.

What can we learn? Once a society has had a deep and sustained encounter with Christianity, it is not easy to remove the Christian residue even if the dogmas of the faith are rejected. Dogmatism outlasts dogma. The idea of heavenly perfection is far more seductive for a post-Christian people than for a people that has always been pagan. A post-Christian society may be especially prone to revolution and therefore susceptible to an authoritarian regime—tricked up, perhaps, in the garb of democracy, which makes the regime more palatable to the citizens and power easier for the leader to wield.

CHAPTER 3

Democracy as Decadence

D emocracy, a movement that was sweeping Europe during his lifetime, provoked Nietzsche's ire. "The democratic movement is the heir of the Christian movement," he wrote, (BGE, 202) and he was convinced that the rise of democracy signaled the decline of humanity.[1]

Nietzsche argued that changes in the conception of God from the Old Testament to the New paved the way for modern democratic movements. The God of the Old Testament was a God of a particular people, a warlike God who took pleasure in smiting the enemies of his people, who demanded blood sacrifices, who was local and particular in his concerns if not his agency. By contrast, the God of the New Testament, like the Jewish people, went wandering and in the process became a cosmopolitan God, a God who loved everyone, a God who viewed all people as equals (AC, 17). Theology, in other words, became democratic as the noble, tribal, and violent

God of the Old Testament became the tame, cowering God of "love your neighbor as yourself" and "turn the other cheek" and "resist not evil."

This shift in the conception of God made possible a change in the conception of man. If God is the God of *all* men, then all men are equal. If all men are equal, then the only legitimate political system is one in which all are treated equally. When all persons are understood to possess equal value before God, the way is paved for the doctrine of equal rights. But if, as Nietzsche asserted, the will to power is the driving force of all life, then the doctrine of equal rights flies in the face of a basic fact of existence. It is, in this light, opposed to life itself. It countenances the equal treatment of the weak and the strong. Women are treated with as much respect as men and given rights equal to men's. Class distinctions and the natural divisions between the strong and weak and between the healthy and sick collapse into a heap of sameness. The strong are hamstrung, and the weak are invited to pretend they are something they are not. This is a recipe, Nietzsche believed, for social decay.

The decadence of democracy manifests itself in several ways that we might summarize as the emergence of weak nomads running in herds. First, people in general become weak. Compelled to defer to the wishes of the majority, they lose their ability to think independently, considering every question in terms of what the majority will think or do. No longer creative, free, and healthy individuals, they are reduced to thinking about their "neighbor." They will voluntarily submit to their own emasculation, even wielding the knife themselves, as they seek solace in the company and approval of others.

These "others" represent what Nietzsche called the "herd." Healthy individuals, men who have not succumbed to the sickness of equality, democracy, Christianity (they are all of a piece), are not afraid of solitude. They are not afraid of pain or of striving for the kind of greatness that sets them apart from, or even at odds with, the crowd. Nietzsche called the gregarious animal of late-stage democratic society "the last man." He seeks a pleasant and peaceful life. He is content with his petty and vulgar entertainments, does not strive to improve himself, and seeks above all to live a long life. He aspires to little more than peace and prosperity. He calls himself happy, but this happiness costs little and requires no sacrifice. The last man avoids risk, pain, and chaos. He is perfectly happy to find happiness in a bottle or a pill (or presumably Facebook), as long as he does not have to think seriously about happiness or about the degraded beast he has become.

Nietzsche believed that all of Europe was, by virtue of this democratic leveling, becoming more homogeneous—not just in culture, but physiologically as well. The nations of Europe were, in a word, ceasing to be marked by their particular racial histories and cultural characteristics. They were becoming a bland mass of last men, a European herd in which greatness was only an embarrassing memory (because great men are dangerous) and happiness was promised to all. European peoples were becoming "supra-national and nomadic." Today we'd say such men are the perfect denizens of a European Union that celebrates the cosmopolitan sameness of a continent without borders, where last men in search of diversion can wander unmolested across frontiers once jealously guarded by proud and distinctive tribes. Keeping watch over them is a single benevolent authority that promises happiness, or at least the possibility of happiness, and equality to all.

Yet equality is hostile to life, and the aspiration to equality and equal rights therefore finds itself beset by a countervailing force. On the one hand, democracy undermines the strong by fostering values such as equality and neighborliness—or in today's parlance, "niceness." Democratic citizens are expected to be nice to each other. Children are admonished to play nicely with their peers. Follow the Golden Rule, we are told. Share with those in need. All of these dispositions, Nietzsche believed, deprive the strong of the very qualities that in a healthy society they would assert.

Nevertheless, the pathological softness that democracy produces cloaks a hidden aspiration that breaks out in unexpected ways. Even in the so-called love of neighbor, Nietzsche found a surreptitious will to power, for in helping my neighbor when he can't help himself, in giving a person something she needs but cannot secure for herself, I am putting my neighbor in my debt. He owes me something, even if only his gratitude. But in Nietzsche's view, the dynamic of debt is really nothing other than the will to power masquerading as goodness, which is to say, asserting my superiority over the beneficiary of my kindness.

The weak of society will naturally tend to seek each other out just as sheep find comfort and security in the herd. Indeed, for Nietzsche, the weak are naturally disposed to congregate, while the powerful naturally stand alone, inclined to separate from the herd lest the pathologies of the herd infect them. For this reason, great men are rare in a democratic age, and at the same time great men are feared, for greatness and power are inseparable. The herd fears nothing as much as a lion who naturally preys on the members of the herd.

Out of this equality social-contract thinkers emerged. Although Thomas Hobbes, John Locke, and Jean-Jacques Rousseau differ in important ways, they are united by the conviction that all men are naturally equal and that the legitimacy of a regime depends on the consent of the governed. The authority of such consent depends on the equality men enjoy in a mythical state of nature. Rather than see political power as emerging from a contest between competing powers, the social-contract thinkers derive legitimate authority from the agreement of all participants to cede part or all of their power to a superintending authority that represents everyone and, by virtue of the agreement, amplifies the power of the individuals in a political body rooted in consent. Power is thus both ceded and claimed, the members of the new state voluntarily submitting to this power that they tell themselves is nothing more than a reflection of their own wills.

Nietzsche argued that the democratization of Europe, exemplified in the language of social contract, has produced last men—essentially nomadic pleasure-seekers—who will pave the way for a tyrant. Last men do not concern themselves with politics or with anything other than their own immediate, hedonistic desires. They are herd animals—industrious workers who do as they are told as long as they receive a regular paycheck. The leveling of society has produced a flattening of aspirations as well. Few are driven by the need to excel, to break out of the herd and assert themselves against the herd or even without reference to the herd. But again, if life is constituted by the will to power, then this great lethargy, this ennui of late-stage democracy, will produce the ideal conditions for the emergence of a tyrant—something that thinkers as diverse as Plato and Tocqueville predicted.

Nietzsche also perceived a subtler inner dynamic that undoes democracy. Life is a struggle. The attempt to bring something to life consists of a struggle against all the forces that seek to deny the creation of something new. Nothing is free. Liberal institutions themselves are bought at a price. Their success means the cessation of the striving that brought them into existence. They "stop being liberal as soon as they have been established," and once they exist, they harm freedom rather than sustain it.

For Nietzsche, freedom is "having the will to responsibility for oneself." It requires a willingness to endure pain and hardship for the sake of independence. Freedom is neither easy nor free. It requires "manly instincts." "The free human being is a warrior." As a practical matter, then, freedom is achievable only by a few (TI, p. 75; BGE, 29). Universal freedom is a charade, a false ideal that can never be realized. And though warlike instincts may have been required for the founding of liberal institutions, once those institutions are in place, they cultivate traits antithetical to those that gave them birth. Liberalism is, for Nietzsche, inseparable from the cultivation of the herd animal.

Liberal institutions, paradoxically, require illiberal ingredients: tradition, authority, a sense of responsibility to future generations. But the success of liberalism has altered the notion of freedom as well as the concept of authority, both of which hasten the decadence that eventually paves the way for a tyrant. The instincts that enabled the building of liberal institutions—a sort of hardness capable of enduring trials and a willingness to sacrifice for a future goal—have been rendered inert by the success of liberal institutions.

Modern liberal democratic citizens desire peace and plenty. They think of freedom as the immediate satiation of their desires rather than "the will to responsibility" and the accompanying spirit of the warrior. Likewise, authority has been transformed. Whereas citizens once willingly submitted to the authority of an ideal or a goal that required sacrifice and perhaps even death, today any authority is seen as a new form of slavery that must be overthrown. The very instincts that make liberal institutions possible are rejected. Liberal institutions suffer the same fate as liberal democratic citizens. They become decadent. They eventually open the door for a new and striking assertion of power that exposes the hollow aspirations of late-stage democratic liberalism (TI, 74-77).

CHAPTER 4

Identity Politics: There Will Be Blood

What binds us together as Americans? In recent years the answer to this question has become elusive. While once there might have been a generally accepted answer, today we are increasingly disposed to give our primary allegiance to a racial or ethnic group with which we identify. In other words, we are coming to believe that what unites us is really our differences, which provide no bond at all. Identity politics unites to divide, and it goes without saying that no nation torn by division, acrimony, grievance, and scapegoating will long survive. But those are precisely the features of identity politics. Nietzsche grasped with stunning clarity the psychology of victimhood and punishment that animates this growing movement in America.

It is important to acknowledge that historical grievances are real. The most obvious stain on American history is slavery, which was introduced to the colonies in 1619—only twelve years after the founding of Jamestown and one year prior to the founding of the Plymouth colony. Slavery was not unique to the United States, of course, nor were other abuses of power, including the subjugation of women and the unjust treatment of native peoples. These injustices are not to be minimized or forgotten. The *way* they are remembered makes all the difference, however, and it is with the subject of memory that we can begin.

Nietzsche argued that memory and unhappiness are inseparable (GM, II, 1). If you want to be happy, you must forget. Of course, forgetting is not easy, especially when the source of your unhappiness constantly intrudes upon your memory. For Nietzsche, pain and memory went hand in hand. Pain is the best mnemonic device—the most effective way to create a memory is to impress it with pain. Obviously, Nietzsche wouldn't have lasted long as a kindergarten teacher.

Constantly recalling past pain keeps it continually present as a persistently festering wound. Unhappiness is the unavoidable result. Human beings remember, and the past is painful. The memory of slavery is painful. Genocide, oppression, and abuse produce painful memories. Memories are burned into the soul and shape it in ways that constantly recall the pain. The soul limps.

While we cannot avoid pain, we can avoid unhappiness by forgetting, which seems to be the prerogative of creatures without a sense of time or a sense of the self. Man's rationality allows him to be unhappy. Nietzsche suggested "active forget-fulness" as a remedy to the unhappiness of memory, but purging oneself of memory is easier said than done, for rationality seems unavoidably tied to memory. Nevertheless, Nietzsche suggested that rationality might provide a solution. Reason developed, he insisted, as an instrument for avoiding pain. If pain and memory are linked, and if reason is a means of avoiding pain, then perhaps reason can provide a means of avoiding memory itself. This, of course, turns on a conception of reason that is quite different from how we generally understand it, for it is difficult to conceive of reason apart from memory. But perhaps reason can provide a means of dealing with pain.

Pain is a fact of existence, and great actions, great achievements, great movements of the soul are impossible apart from sacrifice, which entails pain. According to Nietzsche, great things are begun only with blood, (GM, II, 6) and the human species endures only through human sacrifice (WP, 246). But Christianity, preaching the equality of all, excludes the possibility of human sacrifice. If the species is sustained, energized, and advanced only by means of human sacrifice, then Christianity must bring about the decline of the species. The doctrine of equality runs counter to the facts of existence. It offers an enervating alternative to the will to power.

In paganism, human beings sacrificed other human beings. They might even sacrifice what was most precious—a son or a daughter. During what Nietzsche called "the moral epoch," men sacrificed themselves—that is, their desires—to their gods. The Platonic aspiration to control the appetites and cultivate self-control, declaring war on passion and instinct, is an example of this self-sacrifice, which Nietzsche saw as an obvious decline from human sacrifice. Christianity takes matters a step further. God sacrificed himself for the sins of a guilty people. Sacrifice was not abandoned, but in Nietzsche's view it became absurd. What was once a source of health and vitality now, in this new formulation, produces decadence and the decay of the human species (BGE, 55).

The Christian God does something unnatural: he sacrifices himself for others. In so doing, he declares that he loves all human beings equally and therefore forbids human sacrifice, robbing the strong of the "voluptuous pleasure" of inflicting pain on the weak. When Nietzsche declared the death of God, he reclaimed the possibility of human sacrifice, a necessary condition for the health of the species. The self-sacrifice of God is replaced by a restored pagan will to power. The elimination of God both reclaimed human power and sought to retrieve the human species from the decadence brought about by Christianity.

But what of this pleasure of inflicting pain on others? Are human beings really like that? Nietzsche argued that the presence in every society of strong and weak members produces a dynamic of creditor and debtor. Consider primitive societies.

Ancestors were worshipped as a means of repaying—through some form of sacrifice—a debt owed to them. The sacrifice could take the form of food or honors, but above all the sacrifice was manifested in obedience to customs, laws, and traditions passed down from the ancestors. Obedience was given as a payment due to a creditor. Nietzsche argued that the perceived debt will diminish as the tribe declines and will increase as the tribe becomes more powerful. Ultimately, the ancestors of this expanding and vital tribe will be elevated as gods, and the intensity of devotion rooted in a perceived debt increases dramatically (GM, II, 19).

No one enjoys being a debtor, but most of us are. In fact, most people find themselves in the positions of creditor and debtor at the same time. Consider the following: A man goes to his office, and his boss berates him. In so doing, the boss is exercising his will to power over someone who is weaker. The man goes home and insults his wife. She, in turn, takes out her frustration on their child. The child, not understanding why he has been on the receiving end of his mother's wrath, kicks the family dog. Each person is lashing out at someone or something he perceives to be weaker than himself, and he is doing so as a response to his own perceived weakness. At the same time, each is exercising what Nietzsche called the "right of the masters," which gives him the exhilaration of mistreating someone as "beneath him" (GM, II, 5). In the process, each person gains a kind of relief from the pain he has suffered at the hands of someone more powerful. And the dog is left wondering, "Why did Jimmy kick me?"

Being the victim of abuse, that is to say a debtor, is an indication of weakness. Yet life is the will to power, and Nietzsche showed how even the weak assert themselves by underhanded means, for they cannot face the strong on the open field of combat. In the so-called "slave revolt of morality," the weak subverted the strong by a cunning plot, tricking them into accepting the teachings of Christianity and voluntarily emasculating themselves. Whether or not that is an accurate description of the rise of Christianity, the same psychological dynamic is at work in the attempt by the weak to assert themselves through identity politics and thus extricate themselves from the pain and misery of being subject to another.

Writing in 1888 but sounding as if he were describing twenty-first-century America, Nietzsche identified the etiology of identity politics: resentment, weakness, blame, and scapegoating. It begins with the recognition by the weak that they suffer the "inescapable consequences of a long suppression of the weak by the strong." The next step is to assign the responsibility for their weakness to the strong. Blame has to be shifted. Once the strong are blamed, the weak experience liberation from any sense of responsibility for their own misery: "they threaten, they rage, they curse; they become virtuous from indignation" (WP, 765).

The purity of grievance without personal responsibility unlocks a secret and previously untapped fount of virtue, for what could be more virtuous than a blameless victim? In a society still deeply influenced by Christianity, the role of blameless victim carries special significance, for the blameless victim par excellence is Christ. A Christ-like luster is therefore imparted to the victims, who, blameless and virtuous, are empowered to curse and rage against their oppressors.

Having assumed the mantle of victimhood, they "need the appearance of justice, i.e., a theory through which they can shift responsibility for their existence . . . on to some sort of scapegoat" (WP, 765). This group of self-righteous and deeply aggrieved persons must identify an individual or a group, "a guilty agent who is susceptible to suffering," on whom it can inflict pain and thus gain some relief from the pain of its own weakness (GM, III, 15). Who is the scapegoat? Nietzsche said it could take different forms, depending on the context. It could be God, the social order, education, the nobility—or, somewhat ominously, the Jews. The key, however, is to find an individual or class against which the aggrieved group can vent its aggression, rendered virtuous by blame-shifting. It will express its self-righteous resentment in moral terms: "It is a crime to be born in favorable circumstances; for thus one has disinherited the others, pushed them aside, condemned them to vice, even to *work*."

White privilege is a currently fashionable scapegoat. Some women—and even some men—direct their rage against the so-called patriarchy. In our increasingly Nietzschean age, Christianity itself is fast becoming a scapegoat, for Christianity teaches reconciliation, humility, and above all forgiveness—the very things that would dissipate the energy of identity politics. The virtuous aggrieved must insist that someone else is to blame. Nietzsche channeled their rage: "How can I help it that I am wretched! But somebody must be responsible, otherwise, it would be unbearable" (WP, 765).

None of this is to say that real grievances do not exist. They do. Yet identity politics is precisely the wrong way to resolve historical injustices. It neither forgets as Nietzsche suggested nor forgives as Christianity requires. Identity politics only makes matters worse, for it depends on shifting blame rather than assuming responsibility. It exchanges the real complexities of history for an artificial narrative of the "guilty" against the "pure," the innocent weak against the vile abusers of power. The impulse to alleviate pain by lashing out at another is at the heart of identity politics. Those in pain must locate someone they can deem guilty, even if the "guilty" happens to be merely the descendant of the actual transgressor. Nuance is not a virtue in an age of grievance and revenge.

What is missing is forgiveness, the lack of which prevents the possibility of any resolution, much less reconciliation.

Forgiveness doesn't eliminate guilt, but it does bring an end to the aspiration to inflict pain. Christianity is the enemy of identity politics precisely because one of its central features is forgiveness, which identity politics cannot tolerate. Christianity seeks to reverse the will to power—expressed in identity politics as the will to inflict pain—and replace it with the will to forgive rooted in love for one's neighbor.

Nietzsche thought that forgetting is the only means of alleviating pain. But we must consider whether forgiveness is a more plausible means to the same end. Forgiveness is a means of reconciliation between estranged parties. The estrangement may be the result of deep pain, perhaps pain that goes back for generations. Forgiveness undermines the natural impulse to lash out at the source of one's pain (real or imagined). Forgiveness can end the reciprocal dynamic of blood feuds, of the resentment rooted in violations of rights, of the suffering of innocent victims. To be sure, when we speak of forgiveness in this way, it is difficult not to think of it as a sort of divine power, for forgiveness is nothing short of miraculous when considered in terms of the will to power.

Can forgiveness accomplish the same thing as forgetting? Can forgiveness transcend the pain of memory, the pain of living? Perhaps. But offering forgiveness is not easy, nor is accepting it. Consider Christ's parable of the unforgiving debtor from the Gospel of Matthew:

Therefore is the kingdom of heaven likened unto a certain king, which would take account of his servants. And when he had begun to reckon, one was brought unto him, which owed him ten thousand talents. But forasmuch as he had not to pay, his lord commanded him to be sold, and his wife, and children, and all that he had, and payment to be made. The servant therefore fell down, and worshipped him, saying, Lord, have patience with me, and I will pay thee all. Then the lord of that servant was moved with compassion, and loosed him, and forgave him the debt. But the same servant went out, and found one of his fellow servants, which owed him an hundred pence: and he laid hands on him, and took him by the throat, saying, Pay me that thou owest. And his fellow servant fell down at his feet, and besought him, saying, Have patience with me, and I will pay thee all. And he would not: but went and cast him into prison, till he should pay the debt (18:23–30 [King James Version]).

Nietzschean psychology helps us to understand why the servant acts the way he does. At first glance, we easily see why the servant who was forgiven acts unjustly when he refuses to grant the same kindness to his debtor. But let us consider this story more closely. When the king demands payment of the debt, the servant falls to his knees and begs the king's forbearance. The king agrees and goes further: he forgives the debt completely. The servant, however, does not become debt-free. Instead, a monetary debt is replaced by a debt of gratitude. But this debt is infinitely more pressing than the former, for while the monetary debt was heavy, it required only a finite and external satisfaction: come up with the money, discharge the debt, and the relationship will again be equal. Once the king forgives the debt, how can the servant—short of completely and intentionally forgetting—ever be anything other than a debtor? How much gratitude is necessary? If he ceases being grateful after, say, a year, has he acted justly? No. And because the debt is open-ended and non-material, he finds himself in greater debt after he has been forgiven than before.

If all of life is the will to power, it is easy to see how this act of forgiveness accentuates the power of the king and the corresponding weakness of the servant. The servant, receiving forgiveness after groveling at the feet of the king, must find a means to assert his own will to power. He must kick a dog. In this light, it is unsurprising that he would find his own debtor, insist on full payment, and even physically assault him. He *must* act in this way if he is to relieve himself of the sense of impotence caused by the graciousness of the king. This is the reason that receiving an unmerited gift is so difficult. It is why grace is foreign to human nature. Forgiveness, idealized in the gospel, shows a way out, for the dynamic of forgiveness—both given and received—provides an alternative to the economy of pure power, which cannot get beyond the creditor-debtor relationship.

Nietzsche is right: blood must be shed. The debtor-creditor relationship is real and unavoidable. In Christianity, the demand for blood is satisfied, and forgiveness, if received with gratitude and humility, can end the cycle of violence. The alternative is a continual demand for an outlet for the pressure to sacrifice human life. Nietzsche showed why identity politics is both attractive and a vicious cycle. If God is dead, the gospel is nonsense, and the self-righteous and insatiable rage of identity politics is the obvious—and catastrophic—alternative.

CHAPTER 5

Memory, Monuments, and Manipulation

Although Nietzsche seemed to long for active forgetfulness that overcomes the pain of the past and bestows a sort of bestial happiness on the miserable human species, the fact remains that we remember. Complete forgetting is not a practical option. The haunted past animates identity politics, whose partisans manipulate the past to dominate the present. In this chapter, I want to explore Nietzsche's view of history and consider how history is wielded today as a weapon rather than studied as a source of wisdom or cared for as a precious inheritance.

Nietzsche offered various critiques of history. He was especially hostile to the teleological view of history—the idea that it is moving toward a God-ordained end or climax. If God is dead, there is obviously no God-ordained historical process. There is only life and death, health and sickness. If history promotes life and health, it is useful. If it contributes to sickness and death, it should be abandoned.

Action, which is rooted in passion or instinct, is fundamentally unhistorical, for it springs from a concern for the immediate present rather than an interest in the meaning of the past. Not that an interest in the past is necessarily fatal or even avoidable. History can provide models of greatness or resources that give meaning to the present. History can also be appropriated, molded, and shaped to provide persons or cultures with a meaningful origin story—even if that story is not actually true. Ultimately, an historical mode is necessary for life, but so too is an unhistorical mode. If one lived only with an awareness of the past, action would be impossible, and death would result. On the other hand, a purely unhistorical mode is the life of a beast. For Nietzsche, history serves *human* life. History as the accumulation of mere "objective" facts is deadly, for it undercuts the passion necessary for life. Truth is not a criterion for history. What matters is that history serves the will to life and health—that is, the will to power.

This view of history runs counter to the Christian view. Christianity, which sees the succession of temporal moments as a meaningful whole directed toward a climactic end, can even be said to have invented history. For as long as men have been rational beings capable of memory, they have been aware of a past and in some sense haunted by it—we can repeatedly experience an event through our ability to recall it. But Christianity introduced the belief that history is not a series of events governed by fate or chance but is moving in a certain direction. Augustine, in his monumental work *The City of God*, provides a theological understanding of time that situates the past, present, and future in a cosmic narrative with a beginning, middle, and end: creation, fall, redemption, final judgment. He shows that the entire sweep of cosmic events is a single story. God is the Author of the story, the Creator of the world, the King of the heavenly city, the Law-Giver, the Redeemer of a world infected by sin. At the very center of history is the Incarnation, in which God took on human flesh, lived a perfect life, died a horrific death, and came back to life for the sake of a rebellious people who rejected their Creator and live according to their own wills rather than submitting to the will of their Creator, Sustainer, and Redeemer.

The Greeks, of course, were aware of the past—the Athenians of Plato's day looked back with wonder and reverence to the world of Homer, a world of noble heroes and fickle gods. Their past—embodied in their heroic literature—informed their present. Although the past shaped their values and aspirations, they did not have any sense that the sweep of time itself constituted a grand narrative, much less a divine narrative of redemption. In this sense, the Greeks had a past but no history. Christian theology sees the past in light of a narrative that imparts meaning to the whole. All events have a coherence when they are seen in terms of a directional history rather than discrete instances of life, passion, health, virtue, or some other maker of meaning.

If God is dead, however, history in this Christian sense must be rejected. The habits of mind, fostered in a Christian world, that see cosmic meaning in the succession of temporal events must be abandoned, for if God is dead, history has no grand narrative. History can be mined for materials that support life, but history provides neither "truth" nor a framework for understanding temporal events from a "God's-eye view." There *is* no "God's-eye view." There are only the particular perspectives of individuals and peoples imposing their will to power on the chaotic sequence of meaningless, temporal events. Meaning and significance must be imparted by an act of human will. Any teleological conception of history is necessarily false, or perhaps more accurately, contrary to life and health, for such a view tempts men to imagine that God governs all events. Human choice—which is to say, the will—is merely a mirage, or at least dramatically limited. Passion, will, and assertions of power must be subsumed under the divine will and authority. The result? The death of human passion and will, for submission equals death. For Nietzsche, then, the meaning of history is nothing more than the assertion of human will. The striving is the meaning. The passion is what matters. One may strive and fail. One's passions may be thwarted. Nevertheless, what matters is the life, health, and passion necessary for the striving.

If there is no God, there is no heaven and there is no immaterial soul. There is only biological life. While Nietzsche speaks of the soul, his conception of it is earth-bound and rooted in biological existence. There is no life beyond bodily existence. This materialistic conception of reality led Nietzsche to a belief in what he called the "eternal recurrence" of all things. If the universe is eternal—as in the nineteenth century it was generally believed to be—then every event that could happen has already happened. In fact, every event has occurred an infinite number of times. There is truly nothing new under the sun. What has happened will happen again, over and over, in the eternal recurrence. He recognizes that for some this thought might be crushing—condemning, as it does, all things to the monotonous repetition of every event in an endless sequence from which there is no escape. But some people, he speculates, those who truly recognize the importance of the eternal recurrence, might feel a great sense of relief, even joy. Why? By embracing this view of time, Nietzsche in one respect acknowledges that life itself constitutes the ongoing meaning of history. Even when life begins to decay and civilizations become decadent, the eternal recurrence suggests that a phoenix-like resurrection is approaching. One might also speculate that the relief and joy embedded in this doctrine might come from the denial of any sort of divine judgment, which has haunted the Christian world (and not only the Christian world) for centuries (GS, 341).

There are two problems with this doctrine—one scientific, the other philosophical. First, scientists now affirm that the universe had a beginning and likely will end, a view that does not square with the eternal recurrence (although the speculations of a multiverse would seem to accommodate Nietzsche's scheme). Second, while Nietzsche introduces this doctrine at least in part as an alternative to the Christian conception of history, it is not a simple matter to separate oneself or one's culture from the influence—or the infection—of Christianity. While it is true that in many quarters today God is deemed dead, or has at least been carefully removed from any influential roles, it has not been as easy to eliminate the residue of theistic thinking as it pertains to time itself. God may not be superintending a cosmic narrative leading ultimately to a divine restoration of all things and divine judgment, but most people still hold to some notion—albeit secularized—of progress. Indeed, it might not overstate the case to suggest that modern theories of progress are actually rooted in a Christian aspiration for the kingdom of God, progressives insisting that this kingdom will be realized in time rather than consummated in some eternal state. Progress is a secularized, temporalized eschatological longing born in a Christian milieu and is not easily shaken. Nietzsche's attempt to provide an alternative to a Christian account of time has failed to take hold. Becoming "post-Christian," in other words, is not the same as returning to a sort of pre-Christian paganism. A people once formed by Christianity will reveal the contours of that Christian influence even if it rejects Christian theology. Rejecting the faith is not the same as eradicating its influence. A consciousness formed by Christian categories remains profoundly Christian despite the rejection of dogma, creeds, and practices.

Modern citizens, even modern radicals, who demand equality, tolerance, or respect are speaking the language of Christianity, even if they deny the metaphysics that makes those concepts anything more than the mere assertions of their desires. When these same citizens adopt a doctrine of progress, which is derived from a secularized Christianity, it is likely—perhaps even inevitable—that they will come to see themselves as more virtuous than their ancestors. They will be tempted to judge the past by the standards they hold to be self-evidently true. Rather than extend a measure of tolerance to those who lived before them, they dismiss and even condemn the achievements of the past because of some perceived failure. They are, in other words, strikingly—and stridently— *intolerant* of the past. This is the state of mind now called "wokeness."

Some examples might help to elaborate this point.

In June 2018, the American Library Association renamed the Laura Ingalls Wilder Medal, established in 1954 in honor of Wilder's work, to the Children's Literature Legacy Award. It seems that the universally loved *Little House* books do not sufficiently exhibit the "core values of inclusiveness, integrity, and respect" that the ALA wishes to recognize with this award but "reflect dated cultural attitudes toward indigenous people and people of color that contradict modern acceptance, celebration, and understanding of diverse communities."[1] The terms "dated" and "modern" indicate an unstated though clearly present doctrine of progress. Whereas in 1954 the ALA considered Wilder's work worthy of honor, it now understands that her work lacks the virtues necessary for public esteem. To be sure, the books include some disparaging remarks about Native Americans and African Americans, but the attitudes expressed were not unusual for the period depicted, and it is clear from the tone of the books and even the explicit words of some of the characters that those disparaging views are not condoned. Nevertheless, in the name of tolerance, one particular community must be the subject of special censure, namely, that diverse community we call the past. This censure is possible only if the community of the present asserts its own moral superiority, an assertion that would make Nietzsche wince. But Nietzsche's thought now finds itself wed to a self-righteous moral absolutism that justifies a repudiation of the past.

The same censorious, virtue-signaling absolutism can be seen in the removal of classic works of literature from school libraries because the language of racism or sexism might prove disturbing. When *To Kill a Mockingbird* or *Huckleberry*

Finn is removed from a library, the concern centers around the use of the "N-word," as we now delicately refer to it, which has completely eclipsed the "F-word" in the lexicon of forbidden terms.[2] It is apparently lost on the sensitive censors that in both books racism is condemned and black characters are depicted with dignity. No matter. As in identity politics, there must be a scapegoat, and a price must be paid.

The zeal to obliterate Civil War monuments is another example of the past's being judged and found wanting by the virtuous present. The disconcerting rage directed at memorial statues of Confederate soldiers in Durham and Chapel Hill, North Carolina—toppled and kicked by furious mobs—was not a demonstration of moral relativism. Neither was this vandalism simply a case of moral posturing masquerading as a power play. Such episodes reveal a profound moral absolutism, a profound self-confidence in the righteousness of the cause. Judgment is rendered, and someone or something must pay the price.[3] Monuments to Christopher Columbus have suffered the same fate.[4]

One wonders where the moral rage stops. If the harsh light of judgment were turned on *any* figure in our past, might he not be guilty of violating some jot or tittle of the twenty-first-century code of social justice? And what about us? What will prevent our children from passing the same judgment upon our work? If our descendants find in the record of our thoughts and deeds even a hint of vice, if their understanding of virtue shall have "grown" beyond ours, then all that we have worked for must be torn down and destroyed without mercy or apology. Someone must be to blame. There is no attempt to understand. There is no inclination to forgive. There is only the blindness of self-righteous rage and the destruction that always accompanies it.

CHAPTER 6

OMG! The Weaponization of Language

I t has been said that money is power. Some have suggested that knowledge is power. For Nietzsche, language was a central aspect of power. Nietzsche noted that the "lordly right of giving names extends so far that one should allow oneself to conceive the origin of language itself as an expression of power" (GM, I, 2).

Philosophers have long recognized language as a crucial faculty that distinguishes man from other creatures. Aristotle wrote that human beings, unlike other animals, possess "rational speech," which is, among other things, for distinguishing between the just and the unjust. That is to say, language is employed to make moral distinctions. Language is tied to rationality, which in turn is tied to morality. Language is a means by which human beings can grasp the moral structure of reality which, according to Aristotle, is intelligible.

Plato, whom Nietzsche saw as the fount of many errors, taught that words are metaphysically tied to the objects they name. To name something correctly is to call something according to what it is. Names have meaning, and things possess natures or essences. Words are not merely verbal markers agreed on by a group of speakers. They point to something beyond themselves and can do so well or badly—not just with respect to efficiency but with respect to reality. We see here a distinction between what is called the "nominalist" view of language, in which language is merely the product of an agreement between users to signify an object by a particular word, and the "realist" view, in which words are connected to the nature of the thing they signify.

While not presenting a systematic account of language, the Bible suggests its centrality in human and divine affairs, beginning with the creation narrative in the first chapter of Genesis. In his first positive act, God speaks: "And God said, 'Let there be light.'" Then God "called" the light day and the darkness night. God speaks the creation into existence and then names it.

On the sixth day, "God created man in his own image, in the image of God [*imago Dei*] he created him." Although the text does not explain what that means, we can infer from what follows that the *imago Dei* confers two important powers. First, in the verse that follows the creation of man in God's own image, God gives him "dominion" over all the other creatures. We may conclude, then, that the *imago Dei* includes the prerogative to rule. God gives man authority, and authority implies a hierarchy in which one is ordained to rule and another to be ruled.

In the second chapter of Genesis, God brings all the living creatures of the earth to Adam "to see what he would call them; and whatever the man called every living creature, that was its name." The first human act—naming the animals—parallels the first act of God, which was speaking the world into existence. Man, created in God's image, does the sort of things God does: he rules and names. And the two acts are closely related. To name something is to classify it in relation to other things. To name is therefore to give (or reveal) the meaning, purpose, and relations of the thing named. It is, as Nietzsche put it, "a lordly right," for it assumes a kind of authority over the thing named. It implies power. God asserts his power when he calls the world into being, and man asserts his power when he names the various parts of the creation.

Interestingly, the fall of man, like the creation, turns on language. The first words of the serpent call into question the words of God: "Did God say, 'You shall not eat of any tree of the garden'?" A creature, made by God, uses words, the medium of the creation event itself, to question the words of the Creator. In a remarkable usurpation of the power of language, words are used to induce the man and the woman to act contrarily to the words of God. It is the assertion of the will to power without any submission to that which is right. Right, in this context, is nothing other than a voluntary submission to the ordering will of the Creator.

The woman tells the serpent that if she eats from the tree she will die. The serpent accuses God of lying. Words, which are the means by which order is created and revealed, are here employed in a lie, an inversion of their purpose. And when the woman and then the man eat the fruit of the forbidden tree, they immediately undergo a transformation, becoming aware of their nakedness and seeking to cover themselves. In other words, by entering the world of a lie, by acting contrarily to the order of creation, they come to see themselves outside the harmony of the created order. The result is shame, which they pathetically attempt to cover from the gaze of God, the original source and speaker of order in whose image they have been made.

The Gospel of John begins with a creation hymn that echoes the original creation story. Genesis begins, "In the beginning God created the heavens and the earth." John begins, "In the beginning," and goes on to link the creation event to the divine Word (*logos*), who is Christ: "In the beginning was the Word, and the Word was with God, and the Word was God. He was in the beginning with God; all things were made through him, and without him was not anything made that was made." The Word is the agent of creation. All that exists was made through the *logos*. The first utterance of

God in the Genesis account is "Let there be light." John builds on that theme—"In him was life, and the life was the light of men"—identifying light with life and suggesting that all things have life by participating in the divine *logos*. Words here seem to have life because of their connection to the Word, who is the source of all life. The living Word gives life, which is associated with light, the source of clarity and illumination and the very first thing God creates in Genesis.

The biblical authors are clearly suggesting that language is tied to the source of being itself. Words have a metaphysical reality, and one can participate in that reality either well (truthfully) or badly (lying). To speak truth is to speak words that correspond to the life that ultimately comes from God. To lie is to participate in darkness, which brings shame and death. If language and truth are connected and are given life and meaning by virtue of their genesis in a divine order, and if Christ is the *logos* of God, then lying is, quite literally, anti-Christ.

Nietzsche must reject this account of language, of course. If there is no God, there is no divine source of language. Naming is not a matter of "rightly naming" but of asserting one's "lordly" will over reality. Language, then, is another way to exercise the will to power.

Long before Nietzsche, some philosophers questioned the Platonic-Christian account of language. In his own day, Plato's chief philosophical rivals were the Sophists, who boasted of their ability to manipulate language for the sake of power.

Rejecting Plato's notion that words express universals that have real existence, Thomas Hobbes (1588–1679) argued that the only universals that exist are the words we use to designate universals. Take the word "human," for instance. There is no universal human nature that unites all human beings. The word "human" is merely a conventional binding agent, if you will—a linguistic glue by which all human beings are joined. But if there is no human nature, there is no such thing as a right or wrong way for human beings to act. As Hobbes put it, whatever a person desires he calls good, and whatever a person hates he calls evil. Good and evil are not rooted in the created order but are simply a matter of individual desire.

A student of language, Nietzsche spent a good deal of time considering its nature and origins, arriving at a developmental and naturalistic approach. Primitive man did not possess language and therefore did not possess rationality. Instinct rather than reason was his guide. He lacked memory, and as we have seen, Nietzsche regarded forgetfulness as necessary for happiness. Primitive man also lacked consciousness, which emerged only with the need to communicate with others—specifically, the need for the strong to command the weak (GS, 354). As society developed (and it is not clear what, exactly, prompted such a radical change), instinct was no longer adequate. Men had to become predictable for the sake of living successfully with others. "They were reduced to thinking" (GM, II, 16). Thus condemned to remember, they were also condemned to unhappiness. But in becoming thinkers, men became calculable—that is, predictable. Part of this calculability is the capacity to think in moral terms. A "good" person is one who works well with others, who tells the truth, who plays according to the rules of society. A "bad" person is the opposite. He is an unsociable person, one who refuses to conform to the standards of the herd. Society cannot tolerate his presence, so he must be driven out, or at least quarantined.

In Nietzsche's account, human beings experience a sort of a fall, not by violating a command of God but by becoming rational, conscious, and social. This development produces unhappiness and paves the way for a decline into decadence. Christianization brings democracy, the final stage of decadence. When all are declared equal, greatness is impossible, and the majority is insulated from the powerful aspirations of the few. The will to power is thwarted by the will to congregate, itself merely an instance of the will to power that is exercised by the weak and resentful rather than by those who are proud and strong.

If language does not have a divine origin, then neither does reason. Thus, the conception of *logos* in John's Gospel must be deconstructed. But the connection between language, rationality, and the divine runs deep in the Western psyche. If language somehow touches or points to reality, and if rationality is the term we use to describe the underlying order of that reality—an order that exists, not one we impose—then the concept of truth must be connected to both language and reality. To use language to accurately describe reality is to speak truly. In this context, truth can be seen as divine, for it is an acknowledgment of an order that is not dependent on human will but to which human will must submit. This is a line of thinking that Nietzsche vehemently attacked.

As we have seen, Nietzsche rejected the so-called "will to truth," which depends on a Christian or Platonic conception of reality. Truth is not divine. It is not rooted in a divine mind or a divinely created order. The will to truth must be rejected and replaced with the will to power. But it is not easy to reject truth. Rationality itself seems to depend on the recognition of the category of truth. The law of non-contradiction, at least within the rational ghetto, depends on the notion of truth and falsehood.

If we reject the notion of truth, we call into question not only rationality but also the nature of language, which was hitherto thought to be the conveyor of truth by means of rationality. But "shouldn't philosophers be permitted to rise above faith in grammar?" asks Nietzsche (BGE, 34). He has already compelled us to jettison faith in truth along with faith in rationality. Here we are asked to question grammar itself. He eventually tips his hand: "I'm afraid we're not rid of God because we still believe in grammar" (TI, p. 21). And why must we cut so close to the bone? Nietzsche is trying to remove all vestiges of theism, and the operation must be radical. Reason, truth, and grammar all must be reconceived so that they do not point beyond themselves to a reality made by God. At best they are tools, instruments of power, or perhaps most aptly, weapons.

Language as power. Words as weapons. A rejection of rationality. Could anything better describe our current social and political climate? In 1949, the English novelist and essayist George Orwell published his masterpiece of dystopian fiction, *Nineteen Eighty-Four*, in which he depicts a future society under the absolute rule of Big Brother, whose government rules with an iron fist and seeks to control not only the actions of its citizens but, more importantly, their thoughts. "Thought-crimes" are punished and citizens are compelled to affirm whatever the government declares is true, even if it says that $2 + 2 = 5$.

In an appendix to the novel, Orwell describes the principles of "Newspeak," the official language developed by the political leaders to replace "Oldspeak," which is to say English. Newspeak is intended to limit the range of thought by reducing the number of words and shades of meaning. Each word was given a denotative meaning and all other connotations were eliminated. Additionally, all superfluous words were eliminated, as were all words needed for unorthodox thoughts. Once Newspeak was fully implemented, "heretical thought...should be literally unthinkable, at least so far as thought is dependent on words." In short, if you want to completely control a population, control the language, for rational thought is impossible apart from language. When a word is eliminated from a vocabulary, the concept it represented becomes obscure at best and eventually unimaginable. People cannot act intelligibly without first imagining the purpose and end of their actions. By controlling language, the government controls not merely actions but thoughts that might generate actions.

Protecting the integrity of language requires more than guarding against the nefarious plotting of a Big Brother or resisting the fear tactics of the social justice warriors. In many respects, we are debasing language quite well on our own. Some of our most pervasive technologies have done much to dumb down our language, reducing many of our encounters with one another to electronic huffs and grunts. Twitter, email, Instagram, Snapchat, and the rest prioritize speed over accuracy, substance, and literary style. OMG! ROTFL! NVM. Emoji. Images flashed from person to person at the speed of light and with the foresight of a gnat. We are more connected than ever, but the sociologists tell us we are also lonelier than ever. Could it be that our willingness to bypass the serious work of thinking clearly and expressing ourselves well contributes to this sense of isolation? Surely there is a connection between thinking well, writing or speaking clearly, and listening attentively. A speaker wants to be heard. A writer wants to be read. But hearing and reading are proxies for something more fundamental: understanding. And understanding takes sustained attention. It requires respect for another person's words, which signals respect for the person himself. Linguistic shorthand can, if abused, lead to attention shorthand, which leaves us lonely and longing for the sustained concern and understanding found in true communication. Words matter. Rational speech is one of the attributes that distinguishes human beings from other creatures. We ought to attend with care, and even seek to preserve with love, the linguistic riches we have inherited.

Even if we speak and write well, however, words can still be employed merely as instruments of power. Consider *Rules for Radicals*, Saul Alinsky's handbook for revolutionaries who want to change the world, published in 1971 and supposedly a model for Barack Obama's community organizing projects prior to his meteoric political rise. Alinsky is upfront about his goals: "In this book we are concerned with how to create mass organizations to seize power and give it to the people."[1] And again, "my aim here is to suggest how to organize for power."[2]

Since power is the central theme of Alinsky's book, it is not surprising that Nietzschean themes abound. For example, in an epigraph, Alinsky offers "an over-the-shoulder acknowledgment" to "the first radical known to man who rebelled against the establishment and did it so effectively that he at least won his own kingdom—Lucifer." Alinsky declares, much like Nietzsche, that he hates dogma, which he calls "the enemy of human freedom."[3] He takes a Nietzschean stance against morality in a chapter on means and ends, asserting that if the ends are held in high enough regard and the means are deemed effective, the means are clearly permissible.

This is not to say that moral values are without use. In fact, to be an effective organizer it is necessary to "clothe" one's arguments in "moral garments."[4] Furthermore, the battle is half won if the radical's goals are framed in terms that resonate with the population. Words like "liberty" and "equality" touch a deep chord in the American psyche. Terms like "diversity," "pluralism," and "tolerance" stir many Americans today. Consider the difficulty of arguing against an opponent who has established himself as the champion of freedom. Or the defender of equality, tolerance, or love. All kinds of assertions are made today with the confidence with which one might declare that the earth is a sphere: "Our diversity is our strength." "All beliefs are equal." "Gender is fluid." To challenge these is to run afoul of the keepers of the words. But are these assertions true? Even to ask the question is to flirt with heresy, and heretics don't fare well under Nietzsche's Puritan Warriors.

CHAPTER 7

Life, Death, Sex, Babies, and Gender

F or the past several decades, controversies related to life and sex have been at the heart of the so-called culture wars. This is not surprising, for these questions go to the heart of our understanding of what it means to be human. As that understanding changes—or more accurately, as our views diverge—tensions will increase. Tensions are high because there are competing ideas of what it means to be human. These differences are not easy to resolve, but they can be identified.

In the Christian West, human beings have long been understood to possess an inherent dignity by virtue of their creation in God's image. Men ought to be treated with respect; murder, theft, and lying are wrong. From this understanding emerge doctrines of equality and human rights. This view of the human person begins with a theological claim and builds from there. Remove the theological foundation, and the entire edifice goes wobbly.

From this view there also emerges a certain teleology—that is, an understanding of the design or purpose in nature. Aristotle was able to construct a teleological account of human nature without the benefit of Christian theology, but he did ultimately rely on a divine principle he called the Unmoved Mover. Christians easily appropriated his basic structures and gave a specific name to this hitherto anonymous Mover of All Things. Aristotle and his later Christian appropriators argued that all things are endowed with a nature. A thing thrives by living in accordance with its nature. Man's proper ends include seeking knowledge, having friends, and caring for his children. To revel in ignorance, to live a life without friends, to abuse one's offspring—all of these are indicators of an unhappy, unhealthy life, one ill-suited to human beings. One can ground such an account in a conception of nature, but as Aristotle's work indicates, teleology tends, perhaps unavoidably, toward theology.

In Christian thought, the sexual urge is seen as natural and proper to human beings. It leads to the continuation of the species and fosters the bond between husband and wife, who are charged with caring for the children begotten by the sexual union. These children are, in turn, God's image-bearers, and parents inherit a profound responsibility to raise them so that they too will acknowledge their responsibilities to God, their parents, and future generations.

Sex is therefore natural, but best expressed within limits. Marriage between a man and a woman is the proper context for sexual expression. Sex requires a sort of discipline. It is not simply the expression of love or a source of pleasure but a union of two physically and otherwise complementary persons for the purpose of procreation, communion—and yes, pleasure.

Nietzsche, of course, would have none of this. In denying God, he necessarily denied teleology. He denied that nature is designed with a purpose or that human nature in particular is morally ordered toward definitive ends. There is only the will to power. The strong prevail and the weak submit. There is no good or evil other than this: good is that which serves to secure one's desires, and evil is whatever thwarts those desires (AC, 2).

Nietzsche did not deny that men are men and women are women (he was not into gender fluidity), but he would never acknowledge that sex has a purpose (other than a brute biological one) or that it should be limited to the heterosexual union of marriage characterized by mutual respect. Nietzsche, in fact, often wrote derisively about women. And why not? If life is simply the will to power, and if men often find themselves physically and socially more powerful than women, then why not press the advantage? What rational person forfeits power to those who are weaker? Doing so would be evidence of an addled mind unsuited to domination.

For Nietzsche, marriage is not rooted in love. Or to be more precise, love is not the origin of the institution. It was only in the Christian age—an age of decline—that the sex instinct was restricted to a loving relationship (BGE, 189). Nietzsche sounds like a radical feminist on this point. Marriage "is founded on the sex drive, on the drive for property (woman and child as property), on the drive for *domination*" (TI, p. 76). Power is manifested not only in children but in descendants, in wealth, and influence. A large family is a means of exercising the will to power. Nietzsche even adopts a prophetic mode and anticipates the end of marriage: "modern marriage has *lost* its meaning—consequently, we are getting rid of it" (TI, p. 76). The disintegration of marriage is not a problem, though. Strong people will always find outlets for exercising the will to power, and the sex drive, along with other biological drives, remains unabated. Is there any reason to shy away from rape as a means of practicing domination? In Nietzschean terms, the clear answer is no.

If there is no moral component to human nature and if sex is merely an instinct—an itch to be scratched—and if power lies at the heart of all human relationships, then there is no way to argue that sex ought to be limited to monogamous, heterosexual unions consecrated by a sacramental or covenantal blessing administered by a priest or minister. What matters is not the willing submission to a set of standards handed down from on high or somehow fixed in the created order. What matters in this scheme is instinct and power. If two men find sexual satisfaction by using each other as instruments, fine. Two women? No problem. Multiple individuals? Sure. How about a man and a child? On what grounds can we object? The man has the power and the child does not. Consent, that sacred concept upon which our society puts so much faith, is nothing more than a shibboleth. At best "consent" was a clever invention of the weak to protect themselves against the strong. The sooner the strong recognize that, the sooner they will be able to exercise and extend their will to dominate.

If consent is a false standard, then new and exotic horizons of sexual activity open up. Not only do children become fair game but so too the unwilling objects of one's desire, both human and non-human. What, after all, is a beast but one more entity upon which I can assert my will to power? Many recoil at this thought, but if we embrace Nietzsche's ideas and have the courage to follow his argument where it leads, there is no clear stopping point other than an arbitrary revulsion, which is an indicator of weakness.

Peter Singer, a utilitarian moral philosopher, has made a career of asking hard questions and showing a willingness to follow his premises to their logical conclusions. He burst to fame by arguing that animals (or at least the higher mammals) should be given equal moral consideration as human beings because, like human beings, they can suffer. Singer's foundational moral criterion is just this: suffering is bad. An act that tends to increase suffering is bad, and one that tends to decrease suffering is good. Someone might object: Why is suffering bad and its opposite good? Singer's obvious reply is that we all recoil from suffering. Pain is something that sentient creatures universally abhor. We can invent or imagine other standards for goodness—nature, God, kindness, the Golden Rule, to name a few—but they all fail to compel universally. An aversion to suffering is universal and is therefore the only universal moral criterion.

Singer has argued that limiting man's sexual expression to other human beings is unnecessarily restrictive. There is no moral reason that sex with animals cannot be mutually gratifying, he argues, as long as neither party is injured.[1] But Singer stops short of Nietzsche's conclusion. A utilitarian, he seeks to base a moral theory on sentience and the obvious truth that sentient creatures are averse to pain. His account gets us to some version of equality: Since all sentient creatures are equal in disliking pain, we ought to give each sentient creature moral consideration. "But," Nietzsche would sneer, "why?" If you have the power to assert your will over another, why should you voluntarily limit your power for the sake of another? Why worry about whether another person is hurt in gratifying your sexual urge? Why worry if an animal is injured or killed? The worry itself is an indication of weakness, which expresses itself in the form of pity—a sentiment Nietzsche despises.

Prostitution? This is merely the attempt by two (or more) individuals to get what they want: the john gets sex; the prostitute gets money. They are both exercising their will to power and at the same time acknowledging, by their actions, their lack of power. The john pays because he is afraid of going to jail if he rapes; the prostitute lacks money, which is a form of power, so she (or he) sells something that someone else values. If there were no threat of jail or social sanction, the john would doubtless extract his satisfaction without parting from his money. If the prostitute had unlimited financial resources, she would doubtless find better ways to spend her time than allowing a stranger to paw her.

It goes without saying that pornography opens up a Nietzschean wonderland of power plays. Some prudes lament that women are objectified and debased by pornography. Women are reduced merely to bodies and body parts to be drooled over by lonely men looking for gratification. But is that a problem? The ubiquity of pornography suggests that most have made their peace with that reality. After all, it is said, the "relationship" is consensual (there's that word again). The woman consents to pose for the photographer and acquires money by exploiting the desires of those who purchase the material. The woman, some have argued, is actually the powerful party in the exchange. She is "empowered" by obtaining wealth at the expense of the lonely or bored men who shell out hard cash for a cheap thrill.

But pornography is often combined with violence, to the dismay of some but not of a good Nietzschean. The porn industry seeks to monitor itself for the safety of those who act in films and pose for photographers. They assure audiences that no one was hurt and that hygienic practices were observed. But why? Do they flinch at the last step? Do they show themselves weak just at the moment when the will to power should triumph? Are snuff films really a problem?

The newest rage is lifelike sex dolls that can be fashioned to look like the woman of your dreams. But even better than a real woman, "she" is always available, can be programed to say exactly what you want to hear, and will never get sick or cranky or ask for chocolate. What could be better? Immediate sexual gratification without the trouble of a relationship. It's better than a prostitute, for "she" will live with you and you don't have to worry about the consequences of others playing with your toy. Power? Well, if exercising domination over a cleverly shaped piece of latex is your thing.

In recent years, the so-called LGBT+ movement has made remarkable "advances." Gender, we are told, is not the same as biological sex and is indeterminate. Just because a person lacks a penis doesn't mean "he" is not a man. And a womb is no obvious marker of a woman. Men can have wombs and women can have penises. And you are a bigot to deny such an "obvious" fact. Pronouns, which in a less enlightened age were unproblematic little devices that facilitated clear communication, have become in this brave new world frontline soldiers in a war on nature.

Of course, in Nietzschean terms there is no such thing as human nature. If you strip away every incidental aspect of a human being, what you find at the core is the capacity to will. The essential aspect of one's existence is the capacity to assert one's desires. If you "identify" as a woman today, the world must bend to your desires and employ the proper pronouns. If tomorrow you "identify" as a man or a kitten, the world, so we are told, must conform. Here we get to the heart of the issue. Is there a "givenness" to the world—including our identities and "natures"—to which we must submit, or are we free to make the world whatever we will and expect the cosmos to bow to our desires? In a saner age, the latter view would be considered the height of narcissism. Today it is called liberation. It is a lust for power rooted in the principles of Nietzsche but blended with a Puritanical moralism that turns the entire enterprise into a self-righteous crusade. "I can be whoever or whatever I want to be" (the will to power). "And how *dare* you tell me otherwise?" (moral absolutism).

It is impossible to discuss sex without eventually turning to abortion, for, as the biologists tell us, at least some kinds of sex lead to pregnancy—a persistent reminder of certain irrevocable biological facts. For decades, abortion has dominated our national politics as no other issue has done. Some argue that the unborn are "the least of these," the weakest and most vulnerable persons and therefore deserving of our protection. Some anti-abortion protestors (or should we call them pro-life?—here is a good example of the power of words to move a debate in a particular direction) employ bloody images of aborted fetuses (or babies—again, words matter) in an attempt to shock viewers into concluding that a gruesome crime has been committed. Baby or fetus? Human being or blob of tissue? Autonomous entity or extension of a woman's body? In Nietzschean terms, it really doesn't matter. The will to power governs life. The fetus is seeking power over its mother. The mother is seeking power to do with her body and the fetus as she desires. To feel pity at the plight of the weak is not a virtue but a marker of weakness. As Nietzsche baldly asserts, "A man loses power when he pities" (AC, 7). Abortion is an unambiguous assertion of the will to power. But again, since most abortion advocates prefer to think of the unborn (if they think of them at all) as not fully human, they are clearly seeking to avoid the full implications of their will to power.

Those who favor abortion call themselves "pro-choice," not "anti-life". The primary value behind this label is choice—the capacity to will. My desires must be gratified, even at the expense of another. The language of Nietzschean will to power is inseparable from the language of unfettered choice, which is an assertion that individual will is primary and considerations of justice or goodness or rightness must either fall away or be subsumed under "choice." The absolute rightness of choice is thus elevated as the single and unimpeachable moral principle, and if the essence of a human being is nothing other than the capacity to choose, this elevation is entirely reasonable. What is forgotten in the euphoria of choice is the unborn baby, a helpless human being. Abortion advocates must either deny the humanity of the unborn (a position that is increasingly difficult to maintain) or bite the Nietzschean bullet and acknowledge that abortion is simply about the exercise of power—the strong killing the weak.

Weakness, in a Nietzschean world, is a sign of decline and decay. The weak have no rights, for rights are meaningless if there is no universal human nature or moral structure to human existence. The weak, the degenerate, and the degenerating should, according to Nietzsche, "be shoved under and shoved aside with no mercy whatsoever" (TI, p. 70).

There is one disquieting fact, however, that we all need to face: each of us is going to die. As nature takes its course, each of us will find himself growing weaker, declining physically and mentally. The vibrancy of youth gives way to the dotage of old age. The will to power, so effectively expressed when a man is healthy and strong, slowly diminishes as he slides toward dependency, a "second infancy," and he must be cared for, if at all, by those who are stronger. A so-called "natural death" makes it painfully clear that a man has lost the game. The will to power in the end has eluded him, and his final moments—if he is even aware of them—will bring the crushing recognition that he is powerless.

For Nietzsche, a natural death is grossly unnatural, for the will to power is hopelessly out of reach for the dying man. A natural death is an admission of impotence and nothing more. What an absolute and utter defeat! But Nietzsche discerns a way out, one that proponents of "death with dignity" also look to even if they don't express themselves in explicitly Nietzschean terms—suicide. As he puts it, "Natural death is just death under the most contemptible conditions, an unfree death, a death at the *wrong* time, the death of a coward. Out of love for *life*, one should want a different death: free, conscious, without accidents, without surprises" (TI, p. 71). And so the logic of the will to power is laid bare: unfettered pursuit of desires without the constraint of pity—even pity for oneself.

CHAPTER 8

Creating the Overman: Technology and the Promise of Unlimited Power

I t is impossible to speak of sex and gender without eventually considering the role of technology, which is simply the use of science to amplify power. Today, "Big Tech" is ubiquitous. Google does our thinking, Facebook keeps us connected, the president governs by Twitter, Amazon delivers anything, and everyone seems to have an iPhone. Offering convenience and connection, these companies track our movements both online and off, and they are collecting information about each of us to better "serve" our desires. The resulting algorithms are capable of "knowing" what I most deeply desire and therefore which ads will most appeal to me.

There are programmers who boast of "brain-hacking"—using insights from neurobiology to instill powerful longings for whatever product or "app" they are promoting.[1] That these sophisticated techniques are now aimed at children, whose native defenses are less developed and whose brains are still malleable, is especially egregious. The power of technology is advancing at an unprecedented speed. The iPhone appeared in 2007. Today, smart phones are everywhere. In public and private, our default position is the hunched posture, the nimbly flicking thumbs, and the expressionless downward stare of being "on the phone."

Human beings have always had some form of technology, of course. The word comes from the Greek *techné*, which is translated "craft" or "art." Technology, then, is literally the work of human hands. Human beings are technological creatures; we have always made things for use or for beauty: tools or art. In the seventeenth century, Francis Bacon argued that applied science (another way of talking about technology) increased human power for the "relief of man's estate." Technology was seen as a means to make lives better, happier, less painful. But even in Bacon's time there was another current, less benign and even malicious. In his fable *New Atlantis*, Bacon describes a group of English sailors shipwrecked on a strange Pacific island. They encounter an advanced society ruled by a scientific elite who maintain their subjects' quiescence through technological innovations and careful oversight. On this island, knowledge is tied to power, and though the masses are kept content, they are also kept in the dark. The scientific elite maintain their secrets, controlling the populace through promises of peace and plenty. In Bacon's imaginary realm, "man's estate" is improved, but freedom is diminished. Technology can be used to satisfy physical desires and to control a populace. Power is at the heart of Bacon's project.

We see a similar use of technology today. Most of us have no idea how Google works or how a smart phone is smart, but we cheerfully submit to the technologies that provide convenience, information, and distraction. Bacon, who imagined a powerful though benevolent scientific elite, could never have imagined the degree to which technological powers control human affairs today. Legions of programmers wielding the sophisticated tools of neuroscience and brain psychology are designing hardware and software to ensnare their consumers in mental dependency—for which they gladly pay. This is servitude masquerading as freedom.

On the cutting edge of this technology are the transhumanists, who look forward to uniting man with machine technology—an evolutionary step that will blur the line between the biological and the mechanical. Numerous technologies already tantalize with their promises: mental control of prosthetic limbs that are not connected to one's body, the reception of text messages directly into one's brain, 3-D printable organs, robots that can pass the Turing test, and gene editing. Indeed, the prospect of becoming "more than human" is a heady one. Mortality is a heavy burden. What if through a union of our bodies with machines we could extend our lives indefinitely? What if we could upload our minds so that our conscious existence could continue after our physical bodies had given out?[2]

Although he did not foresee the literal integration of machines and bodies, Nietzsche did descry the diminishment of human beings as they became integrated into the machine economy. Unlike the transhumanists, Nietzsche thought making men more machine-like was a setback—not a victory. Voicing concerns expressed by Marx a generation earlier, Nietzsche asserted that "mankind will be able to find its best meaning as a machine in the service of this economy." Human beings will become cogs in an economic machine that will increase in power even as they are diminished and exploited. Yet this "transformation of mankind into a machine is a precondition" for the emergence of a higher form of humanity as a reaction (WP, 866). This "higher type," this "stronger species" is Nietzsche's notorious *Übermensch*—the "Overman."

Nietzsche contrasts the Overman with the "Last Man." The latter is diminished, small, and weak. He is content to be part of the herd. He is satisfied with petty pleasures and wants nothing more than a long, peaceful life and a quiet death. The Overman, on the other hand, goes beyond. He aspires to the heights—to the pain, cold, and suffering through which great and creative acts can be accomplished. The Overman is beyond good and evil. He strives to get beyond himself, for he recognizes that herd-like humanity is contemptible.

One day the Overman will look back on man as he is now with an embarrassed laugh, just as men today feel a sense of embarrassment when they consider that they came from apes

(Z, Prologue 3). The process is painful, but Nietzsche was convinced that this new kind of man must emerge. The transformation will not be democratic. Not everyone becomes an Overman, who represents a "higher form of aristocracy" based not on the accident of birth but on the capacity to wield power—and not simply power over others, but power over himself as well (WP, 866). For Nietzsche, "not 'mankind' but overman is the goal!" (WP, 1001).

There are elements of the Overman in the transhumanism of our age, which aspires to advance from an inferior state of humanity to something better. An important difference is that the transhumanists aspire to democratic equality—this is for everyone!—whereas Nietzsche found in this impulse the residue of Christianity. His Overman is no democrat. Equality is an aspiration of the herd, for which strength is terrifying and greatness an offense.

The technology that the transhumanists hope will advance mankind is a product of modern science. That's a problem for Nietzsche because modern science is itself the product of Christianity. Nietzsche noted that science initially was motivated, at least partly, by a theological concern: "It was by means of science that one hoped to understand God's goodness and wisdom" (GS, 37). Isaac Newton exemplified this approach to science. Even Voltaire, who was hostile to Christianity, believed that since there was an "intimate association of morality, knowledge, and happiness," the advance of scientific knowledge would make men both morally better and happier (GS, 37).

Today, however, in the wake of God's death, it makes no sense to look to nature for signs of God's goodness (GS, 357). Rather than seeing in nature the fingerprints of God and therefore his providential hand guiding history and marking the way toward holiness, Nietzsche saw only the work of chance (TI, p. 55). Science, born of Christianity, therefore had to be overcome and replaced by a more suitable alternative: scientific atheism (GS, 357). Science, as Nietzsche construed it, is predicated on the nonexistence of God, but this requires stripping away the vestiges of theism that cling to it, the most important of which is the will to truth (GM, III, 24). This transition, of course, will take time, for science and scientists remain deeply infected by the will to truth even though a commitment to truth undermines even more vital goals. The will to truth can be explained only as a metaphysical commitment rooted in theistic belief. Once God is declared dead, the metaphysical structure that gives force to the will to truth is eliminated and men can once again see with clear eyes. The will to power must replace this deeply flawed commitment to truth.

Early modern science was, of course, not a wholly Christian endeavor. While theism and its corollary, the will to truth, were part of the motive for the development of modern science, there was another less savory motive at work. Nietzsche put the matter in the form of a question: "Do you really believe that the sciences would ever have originated and grown if the way had not been prepared by magicians, alchemists, astrologers, and witches whose promise and pretensions first had to create a thirst, a hunger, a taste for hidden and forbidden powers?" (GS, 300).

C. S. Lewis made the same argument in his little book *The Abolition of Man*. Modern science and magic were, he argued, born of the same impulse, namely the subjection of nature to human will. Alchemy sought to turn base elements into gold. Its only problem was that it didn't work. Applied science—that is, technology—sought to subdue nature and met with stunning success. The impulse behind both was the same: the will to power. Lewis admitted that for most scientists the love of truth was stronger than their love of power, but we should never lose sight of the persistent presence of that latter love. And if the love of truth is ever abandoned—as Nietzsche insisted that it must be—then the only game in town is power, which is precisely what Nietzsche predicted. Lewis recognized the implications: man's conquest over nature would lead to some men's conquest over other men.

A good example of how technology, made possible by scientific advances, insinuates itself into our thinking and shapes our behavior is advertising, which often tells us more about ourselves and what we love than about the merchandise it is promoting. With advertising, creative people exercise the will to power by promising that parting with your money will secure power, prestige, or happiness.

In 2013, Sprint rolled out a thirty-second advertisement for its "unlimited" data plan that beguiled its viewers with the slogan "I am Unlimited."[3] The ad's opening words—"The miraculous is everywhere—in our homes, in our minds"—identify the miraculous with technological advances, the apparently magical works of technicians who invent devices and applications that most of us don't fully understand. No longer is the term "miraculous" reserved for God and his works. He is, after all, safely dead. The miracles all around us—even in our homes and our heads—are the product of human ingenuity. And like the biblical Bartimaeus, we open new eyes on a world bursting with wonders.

Two seconds into the ad, the word "unlimited" flashes on the screen. Could the miracles be unlimited? What a world! This promise is delivered by our own hands, or rather by the hands of those few who wield the magic wand of technological power.

The ad continues: "We can share every second in data dressed in pixels." In other words, we can reduce the complexity of a human life to digitized bits. Conceiving of reality in simple, discrete parts, we are tempted to imagine that reality is reducible, comprehensible, and controllable. Echoing the cry of Nietzsche's alter ego Zarathustra—"I beseech you, my brothers, remain faithful to the earth, and do not believe those who speak to you of otherworldly hopes!"—we deny the metaphysical reality beyond human control or even knowing (Z, Prologue 3).

Sprint breathlessly promises that its unlimited data plan will unleash "a billion roaming photojournalists uploading the human experience," implying that the human experience is uploadable. But is it? If we think of the human experience as something that can be uploaded, we alter both the experience itself and how we conceive of it. The experience is changed when we stop appreciating it for what it is and think of it as something we can capture, as something we can control and therefore command. The sheer wonder of an experience is at least partially altered when we imagine we can upload it, re-experience it repeatedly, and share it with friends and strangers alike. Does this sense of control reflect our enhanced powers or our diminished sense of humility—and perhaps even reverence?

"I need to upload all of me," the ad's narrator declares. For some (and I hope many), this is just creepy. But what is being appealed to? What is being assumed? The "need" to upload all of oneself could be a perverse impulse to display oneself to a world of potential viewers—an exhibitionist's dream—or hunger for immortality. I "need" to upload "all of me" so that none of me will be lost. In either case, the "need" represents a longing to transform the human experience through the "miracle" of technology.

The ad closes with the brash assertion, "I need—no, I have the right to be unlimited," and the slogan "I am unlimited" again flashes across the screen. The music and the message reach their climax, and the audience is ready to stand and cheer, or at least switch to Sprint's data plan. Either way, power has been gainfully employed.

There are at least three assumptions behind this advertisement. First, the visible world constitutes the essence of the human experience. The "real" is the tangible, which can be captured by a camera and pixelized. The implication is that the world of thought and idea, the world of spirit, is unreal or at least unimportant, for God and the human soul cannot be reduced to pixels. In a curious twist, the new "miraculous" has rendered the old miraculous unimaginable and therefore unbelievable.

Second, the prevalence of the language of rights in our social and political culture has prepared the way for a claim like the one in this ad. We have become accustomed to speaking and thinking in terms of rights, yet we have neglected what a right implies—the duty of someone else to refrain from coming between me and that right, or that someone else might even have a duty to ensure that I can enjoy the right. But the language of rights slides quickly into the language of sheer desire, giving the desire an apparent moral legitimacy that a mere burst of appetite lacks. This is precisely what we should expect in this age of Nietzschean Puritanism. The language of rights is a residue of our Christian past, but stripped of its proper content, it bestows on our desires an aura of moral legitimacy, validating our bald assertions of power.

The third assumption is just this: "I have the right to be unlimited." In our cultural moment, the idea of limits is offensive. Limits suggest that my desires can—and perhaps should—be thwarted. But who has a *right* to do that? By what authority— social, natural, or divine—can my desires be hemmed in, circumvented, or directed? If the miraculous can be delivered through technological innovation, there is little reason to believe that the miraculous itself is limited or even beyond human control. Indeed, we are the gods of a brave new world where miracles are for sale in the form of electronic devices, where appetitive desire is dressed in the language of rights, and where limits are an affront. If God is dead, any attempt at self-limitation is self-emasculation. I have a right to be unlimited, and that right is merely an indicator of the power I can marshal to assert whatever I desire. Technology becomes the steroid that massively amplifies the will to power.

CHAPTER 9

"Higher" Education and the War on Reason

S omething strange is happening on our college and university campuses. The institutions that used to intro-
duce students to the best books and ideas of our culture
have become swamps of ideologically radical (not to mention
nonsensical) courses, politically correct jargon, irrational
protests, and safe spaces protecting fragile students from any
idea that might make them uncomfortable. At the same time,
the cost of this "higher" education has skyrocketed even as
young people are told that a college degree is essential for any
kind of professional success. So more and more people are
wasting four years in the intellectual playpens of higher education and assuming massive debt for the privilege.

Is there a Nietzschean angle to the hijacking of higher
education by ideologues who are more concerned with their
social and political agendas than with the pursuit and trans-
mission of truth? When we state the problem in those terms,

the Nietzschean themes become obvious. Nietzsche's only sustained engagement with the topic of education was a series of lectures he delivered in the spring of 1872, when he was twenty-eight, titled *On the Future of Our Educational Institutions*. They suggest that he had not yet fully embraced the most radical implications of his thought, and he never consented to their publication. Nevertheless, they give us some sense of his early understanding of the purpose of education and his disdain for modern educational institutions.

In brief, Nietzsche was concerned that the trend toward universal education would lead not to universal enlightenment but to barbarism (EI, p. 17). A growing focus on utility and specialization signaled the demise of truly liberal education (EI, p. 16, 18). These shifts represented the "curse of modernity" (EI, p. 54), a new barbarism marked by concern for "individual personality" rather than the development of the genius of a few great souls (EI, p. 27, 51). True education is necessarily aristocratic, and its focus is on "the only true homeland of culture: Greek antiquity" (EI, p. 31). With the democratization of education came an increasing interest in the practical application of knowledge rather than the pursuit of knowledge for its own sake. Well before Nietzsche's time, this turn toward the practical was expressed in terms of power. Francis Bacon, as we have seen, argued that knowledge should be understood as power over nature. Nietzsche's eventual view of life in terms of power suggests that he came to the same conclusion as Bacon, though by another route and in a far more systematic and far-reaching way.

After those lectures, Nietzsche left us only scattered references to education in his writings. Near the end of his career, he offered the conventional observation that the purpose of education is to see, to think, to speak, and to write. He expressed the same pessimism that marked his youthful lectures when he complained, "There is no concept of [thinking] in our schools anymore" (TI, p. 48). Nietzsche prided himself on his thinking and writing, so this lament is perhaps not surprising. But since the will to power had become a central theme in his work, we should expect power to lie at the heart of the mature Nietzsche's account of education.

We see hints of this in a comment he made about parents and children: "Invariably, parents turn children into something similar to themselves—they call that 'education.'" (BGE, 194). Why would parents do this? To Nietzsche, the answer is obvious: "Deep in her heart, no mother doubts that the child she has borne is her property; no father contests his own right to subject it to *his* concepts and valuations" (BGE, 194). Here the will to power is at the heart of the parent-child relationship. The parents seek to impose their values upon the child, and this imposition they call "education."

The same motive, Nietzsche said, is found in teachers. They are not driven by a love of truth or a "drive to knowledge," but like all human beings, and indeed all living creatures, they are moved by the will to master. Knowledge for its own sake is a false ideal. Knowledge, learning, and education are a means to assert oneself, to dominate. The teacher seeks to promote his family, make money, or acquire political power (BGE, 6). In other words, scholars employ knowledge of their particular subjects to gain power over others.

It might be helpful at this point to consider two very different conceptions of education, for only when we see the options can we understand what is at stake and what a distinctly Nietzschean turn higher education has taken. For the sake of convenience, I will call the older approach classical, as opposed to the radically different approach that I will call modern.

Classical education was characterized by a pursuit of the good, the true, and the beautiful based on a particular conception of reality we have seen in previous chapters. The cosmos is an intelligible whole that is infused with moral categories. The good is not something we make up, not a product of individual or corporate will, but a fundamental characteristic of reality—a reality that human beings can discover and to which they can (and should) submit. Goodness is a constitutive element of reality itself. To know the good is to know that which is true, for truth is merely a mark of reality. Our minds are equipped to know reality, and though we cannot know it fully, we can know truly. And knowing itself is good. Furthermore, reality is infused with a beauty that, again, human minds are capable of perceiving. As we open ourselves to the beauty of reality, we see the coherence of all things; we see connections between particulars, and we see how everything ultimately points toward the divine, who is the source of all things. To pursue the good, the true, and the beautiful is to pursue God. We move upward from the particulars, discerning their order and relationships, ultimately converging in God. From there we move back down from the universal to the particulars, coming to see with clearer eyes the meaning—which is to say the goodness, truth, and beauty—of the particulars now illuminated by the light of God. Classical education is the pursuit of the highest things, predicated on the existence of a hierarchy that we can grasp and ascend. In the process, we come to see how all things are related and infused with divine meaning.

Classical education is often associated with what used to be called a "liberal" education (from the Latin *liber*, "free"), an education suited to free citizens, in contrast to a "servile" education, the narrowly technical training intended, in the ancient world, for slaves. A liberal education was thought to be a necessary condition for self-government, which begins with governing one's own appetites. A beast is subject to its appetites, whereas a well-functioning human being subordinates his appetites to higher things, making self-government possible. A society of self-governing persons can govern its corporate affairs wisely.

A liberally educated person considers fundamental ideas such as the nature of justice, the best kind of human life, and the best kind of society. It is dangerous for slaves to think about such things. Slaves were trained to focus exclusively on a specific job, which would keep them absorbed in their mundane tasks. When they were not at work, they were distracted by entertainments that, like their work, prevented them from thinking seriously about serious matters. They were deprived of the tools and the time for serious reflection, for the last thing a society needs is discontented slaves.

In a democratic society, however, all citizens need to be capable of self-government. That means that all citizens must, at least to some degree, be willing and equipped to think clearly about justice, the good life, and the good society. All citizens must have some access, either formally or informally, to an education suited to free citizens. All must have at least the basics of a liberal education and not be merely trained for a narrow occupation. A nation of servilely educated citizens will be ill-equipped for democratic self-rule.

Modern education is not liberal and often not even servile. Many college professors use words like "truth" only ironically, and they scoff at notions of objective morality and beauty. The entire landscape of higher education appears to be the scene of a sweeping victory for Nietzsche. We have gotten beyond good and evil; we have rejected the notion of objective truth, and we have come to believe that beauty is nothing more than individual preference.

But things are not that simple. Deeply influenced by their Christian past, Americans find it virtually impossible to rid themselves of the residue of Christianity. On many college campuses, Nietzsche's Puritan warriors have taken over, and we see the devastating effects of the will to power married to a moral absolutism lacking any justification other than individual will subconsciously energized by a rejected Christian past.

Consider the frequent protests and violence intended to silence those whose views deviate from the reigning orthodoxy. Consider the unwillingness to engage opponents in rational debate. Rationality, we are told, is merely a contrivance of the white patriarchy to assert and maintain control, which is clearly illegitimate and must be deconstructed. The protesters rely on force, power, and volume rather than arguments. Truth is not the issue. What really matters is justice, equality, and tolerance. And they will destroy you if you disagree or get in the way.

But it is precisely where the moral claims are most strongly asserted and where the will to power is most emphatically embraced that we can begin to see cracks in the logic of the whole noisy enterprise of modern higher education. Although power is asserted with the self-righteousness of a crusader and with an air of supreme confidence, it is a fragile power masking a surprising weakness. Consider the popularity of so-called "safe spaces" and the insistence on "trigger warnings." Safe spaces are designated areas where a person can be assured that he or she (or "they," if you prefer) will not encounter any ideas that make them feel uncomfortable. However, as any sane person living in a free society knows, the world is full of diverse ideas and people espousing them, and some of those ideas will challenge one's own. Higher education was once seen as an opportunity to encounter new ideas, to understand them, and perhaps be changed by them. At the very least, encounters with strange ideas would bring a student to a better understanding of his own ideas. The demand for safe spaces and "trigger warnings"—by which certain ideas and books are quarantined—is a sign of mental and emotional fragility, an unwillingness or even inability to deal maturely and thoughtfully with differences, making tolerance impossible, for people tolerate only what they disagree with. Rather than assume that students are adults (or nearly so) and therefore mature enough to handle challenging ideas, teachers coddle students, insulating them from ideas that might contradict their prejudices.

Nietzsche, who regarded complaining as a sign of weakness, would have despised such delicacy (TI, p. 69). But wait—if the will to truth doesn't matter, if the will to power is the central feature of life, then perhaps these "delicate" students are on to something. Why listen respectfully to someone with whom you disagree? Listening requires seriously engaging with arguments, sifting through them to determine which are compelling and which are not. In other words, respectful and engaged listening is predicated on the idea that truth is a good worth pursuing even if people ultimately differ in the conclusions they draw or the practical implications of those conclusions. But if Nietzsche is right and the will to truth must be replaced by the will to power, then shouting down your opponents—even your professors—makes sense. So does insisting that uncongenial views be silenced and driven from the field. The tactics merely represent the logic of the will to power. Maybe Nietzsche would approve after all.

There are, however, two reasons that these campus protests and movements, while exhibiting some of the characteristics of the will to power, are un-Nietzschean. First, protests and mass movements in the name of equality and tolerance express nothing more than the debased desires of the herd. These students are terrified of greatness, of excellence, of anything other than superficial differences. They demand equality and tolerance while they stifle those who are different, who threaten their comfortable little worlds built on self-righteous platitudes and assertions of solidarity with others who pride themselves in their "radical" thinking even as they cower in conformity. Is there any space for conservatives in this brave new world of tolerance? Please. How about for the old-fashioned liberal who believes in the power of ideas and that vigorous debate is the best means of ascertaining the strongest argument? Increasingly unlikely.

The second reason these movements are un-Nietzschean is that they are charged with a hyper-moralism. Equality must be pursued because it is a self-evident good. So too tolerance, diversity, individual rights, and democracy. How could anyone question the unimpeachable goodness of these ideals? There is no suggestion here that anyone has gone beyond good and evil. Instead, we see a rigorous moralism that would make Cotton Mather blush. These students are so sure of the righteousness of their causes that they are willing to silence any who challenge them. The will to power has been combined with unyielding moral claims. Christianity having been rejected, however, those moral claims rely on mere assertions of will.

Students are not the only ones deeply implicated in this pseudo-Nietzschean charade. Members of the faculty—who should be the mature adults pointing students toward truth—all too often promote and even lead the protests. But this raises another puzzling question: If all of life is the will to power, why would professors seek to empower students in self-righteous rage? Isn't my power what matters? Isn't it ill-advised to empower others who might at any moment turn on me? Why would Nietzsche himself write books that seek to alert his readers to the creeping malady of Western society? Isn't that an act of altruism and generosity rather than an assertion of power?

I don't want to speculate about Nietzsche's motives, but today's radical faculty members are easier to read, for their rhetoric and their deepest commitments give them away. However emphatic their atheism, they cannot cleanse themselves of their residual Christianity. Many are openly hostile to orthodox Christianity, which they blame for injustice, intolerance, and small-minded bigotry. They have, so they say, progressed beyond childish religious belief. They are interested in overturning systemic injustices, in deconstructing power, and in overturning the patriarchy or white hegemony or whatever. They think of themselves as radically and unapologetically democratic, lovers of freedom, committed to ferreting out and purging any person, institution, or idea that contradicts those ideals. They seek to empower the dispossessed, which from a Nietzschean perspective is empowering the herd.

"Woke" faculty members imagine they are powerful agents of liberation, justice, and equality. But again, why empower the herd? Why promote democracy? By what means can equality be meaningfully asserted? These ideals emerged from Christianity, and they make sense only if the human person has an inherent dignity. Democracy, rights, equality, and even the notion of a scapegoat—a concept necessary for identity politics—all find solid grounding in a Christian view of the world. Divorced from that view, those notions are merely blind assertions, claims rooted in the will to power, lacking the moral force that their modern adherents assume they possess.

From a Nietzschean perspective, it makes no sense to empower others unless you believe that in so doing you are empowering yourself. Faculty members who encourage student radicals might be doing so for purely selfish motives. If so, they are seeking to distract impressionable students into thinking herd power means something when in reality it is the pathetic clamoring of the impotent. Few faculty members go this far. Instead they imagine themselves the missionaries of a new age of equality and tolerance, ushered in by the power of protest, revealing themselves to be willing disciples of Nietzsche and unwitting disciples of a desiccated Christianity. Nietzsche would call them craven fools who are unwilling to take the final leap and discard the Christian ideals whose foundations they have sought so assiduously to destroy.

CHAPTER 10

Going Full Nietzsche: Do You Have the Guts?

I t is impossible to understand the radical left in America without recognizing that it is the product of a grotesque combination of the Nietzschean will to power and the moralizing absolutism of a Puritan heritage explicitly rejected but tacitly (though only partially) embraced.

An obvious question is whether this union is stable, let alone coherent. Let us first, though, briefly review the salient attributes of what we have called Nietzsche's Puritan Warriors. They have inherited from Nietzsche a hostility to historical Christianity. God, if not explicitly denied, is at least safely sequestered behind the rhetoric of "my God," a creature of my imagination who never does or commands anything unpleasant, rather than the omnipotent Creator of the universe. There is no Trinity, for if Jesus Christ were divine, then the entire gospel story of his death and resurrection to save sinners(!) would be uncomfortably relevant.

If God is dead or at least out of the way, Nietzsche's world-view becomes plausible, and perhaps even obligatory. Morality rooted in divine command or inherent in the created order has to be dead as well, so we need a different justification for our impulses to action. We can, with Nietzsche, reduce human motives to instinct combined with a will to power—power over nature and power over others. This account provides no notion of legitimate power, the just use of power, or the abuse of power. For Nietzsche, evil is nothing more than weakness and good is nothing more than power. Happiness, then, is the feeling one experiences when power increases, and unhappiness is the feeling one experiences with diminishing power (AC, 2).

The Puritans, for their part, have bequeathed a three-fold legacy to the radical left: (1) egalitarianism, (2) an inclination to think, speak, and act in morally absolutist terms, and (3) a determination to punish those who defy orthodoxy. Each element of this legacy, derived as it is from Christianity (though often deformed), is incompatible with basic Nietzschean assumptions. That is not to say they cannot be simultaneously affirmed—human beings often affirm incompatible positions—but the combination of Nietzschean will to power and moral absolutism is especially incoherent. A society that tries to affirm both principles will suffer cognitive dissonance and, perhaps inevitably, social disruption. The fruits of this chaotic union are apparent in the frequency of violent protests on university campuses and elsewhere.

Nietzsche deplored the principle of equality, and he understood that it emerged from Christianity. To insist on equality while denying the theological account that makes such a demand intelligible is to reduce equality to a mere preference, nothing other than a bald assertion of collective will. If the majority decides that inequality is preferable, there is no way to deny the "rightness" of that new view. Unless a minority proves stronger than the majority (a sign of the end of democracy), the will of the majority must prevail, even if the minority suffers. If the will to power is all there is, then equality is foolishness, an unwarranted concession by the strong to the weak. Such a concession, in turn, unmasks the weakness of those who purport to be strong.

The moral absolutism of the social justice warriors is anti-Nietzschean but profoundly Christian. The radicals who demand equality, tolerance, or justice do not believe that morality is reducible to personal preference, nor are they speaking (or just as often shouting) as moral skeptics who deny the reality of moral claims. On the contrary, they propose a sweeping moral vision of stunning intensity. They are absolutely convinced that racism has thoroughly infected American society and that it is their moral duty to root it out. They are absolutely convinced that poverty is a question of justice and that individuals and governments must alleviate the plight of the poor. They are absolutely convinced that the white patriarchy is an affront to the dignity of the oppressed and must be overthrown. They are absolutely convinced that a woman has a right to terminate her pregnancy and that those who would thwart her are violating the moral space that a woman should enjoy and must demand.

All of these demands are framed in morally absolute terms, and those who make them are not interested in traveling with Nietzsche "beyond good and evil." Nietzsche, for his part, would despise these claims. There are no moral grounds for denouncing racism, poverty, injustice, or the violation of human rights, for he has discarded the very idea of rights. In short, the moral demands of the social justice warriors are undermined by their metaphysical skepticism. They want to have both their skepticism and their social justice. Nietzsche would scoff at their latent Christianity, to which they cling as a child clings to his security blanket.

Social justice warriors are nothing if not self-righteous. They thirst for the punishment of the unjust. They hear with compassion the cry of the innocent victim. And since there can be no divine justice, for God is dead, they arrogate to themselves the authority to mete out punishment upon those who thwart the ideals of equality and tolerance or who violate the rights of approved victims. Justice must be done, and justice demands blood. In a ritual that mirrors crucifixion, the guilty perpetrators of injustices taking the place of the guiltless Christ, propitiatory blood is spilled (usually metaphorically but sometimes literally). White males are made scapegoats with increasing frequency. All the better if they are hetero-sexual. Better still if they are orthodox Christians, for what better exemplifies the oppressive class in the West than that deplorable combination? But while they borrow moral catego-ries from Christianity—guilt, innocence, sacrifice, scapegoat—the absence of Christ dooms the exercise to perpetual frustra-tion. How much punishment is enough? When will the social justice warriors desist, satisfied that the guilty have paid for their sins? When will they offer forgiveness and seek recon-ciliation? The answer is never. In this desiccated Christianity without Christ, no amount of blood is adequate. The stain of guilt is never removed. It is identity politics all the way down.

Given the contradictions inherent in Nietzschean Puri-tanism, why not seek a more coherent position? One option is to discard the Puritanism and go full Nietzsche. There is a bracing attraction to this alternative, though we must consider what we must jettison if we choose this path, for as Nietzsche so clearly understood, his way requires a radical revaluation of everything.

The first to go are the ideals of the good, the true, and the beautiful, which have permeated Western thought and prac-tice. If God is dead, they are merely the imagined ideals of dreamers or perhaps weapons devised by some to gain power over others. We must also rid ourselves of other related ideas that, for better or worse, have shaped our political and social life. This is where the practical implications of Nietzsche's project become clear and the social justice warriors prove far less radical than they imagine themselves to be.

Equality, a principle that today is virtually unimpeachable, has no place in Nietzsche's vision. If all of life is the will to power, then equality is antithetical to life itself (GM, II, 11). Indeed, Nietzsche regarded the social leveling that swept Europe in the nineteenth century as the greatest imaginable danger (GM, I, 12). Why would anyone promote equality? Who in his right mind would elevate the weak, the inferior, and the powerless? The answer, obviously, is the weak, the inferior, and the powerless. The weak long for the security of the herd. Conformity provides a sense of collective power to those who on their own are powerless. In the herd, greatness is feared, for it threatens to expose the weakness of those who have taken refuge in the comforting arms of the group.

The principle of equality assumes that every human being, regardless of race, class, or sex, has an inherent dignity—and therefore enjoys certain rights—simply by virtue of being human. That inherent dignity is difficult to justify without an account of the human person that explains why he is intrinsically valuable. The doctrine of *imago Dei* does that, but Nietzsche has eliminated God. And apart from some metaphysical or even theological grounding, it is not obvious that the idea of human rights makes any sense at all. Nietzsche understood this, asserting that a society enamored with the language of equal rights has set the stage for its own decline.

Strength, power, vitality, and the will to dominate know nothing of equal rights. They know only the voluptuous pleasure of domination.

It is easy to imagine, then, how Nietzsche would respond to the #MeToo movement, which was provoked by highly publicized allegations that powerful men had abused their power over women by seeking sexual favors, either through outright assault or through harassment. Nietzsche would regard this movement as one more indication of the growing weakness of Western culture. The supposed obligation of the strong to respect the weak is a conceit generated by the false ideal of intrinsic human dignity. Once that ideal is overcome, it only makes sense for the strong to assert themselves. What else does strength do? What is power if it is not used? In Nietzschean terms, #MeToo is an attempt by the weak to assert power over the strong through guilt and shame. If successful, it will result in a transfer of power to the weak and the degradation of society as a whole.

#MeToo activists talk about "empowerment through empathy," which smacks of "the religion of pity," (GM, III, 25) for Nietzsche a clear indication of cultural decay. The weak priestly class overthrew the strong warrior class of the Roman Empire, Nietzsche would argue, (GM, I, 8) with the same politics of pity. To a Nietzschean, #MeToo's plaintive cry against oppression is a demonstration of weakness. The abuse of a woman by a powerful man is evidence of her weakness, and she should not be surprised that the powerful try to dominate her. If you are going to follow Nietzsche, you will have to bite this bullet.

Another virtually untouchable political dogma is tolerance. But like rights, this notion is closely connected to equality, for it is based on the assumption that all persons deserve respect—even if we disagree. In Nietzschean terms, however, only the weak practice tolerance. The strong dominate, their happiness enhanced by the effectiveness of their power. Tolerance is an ideal promoted only by the powerless.

Many social justice warriors now seem to embrace the Nietzschean contempt for tolerance despite their veneer of Puritan moralism. Shouting down those who express "offensive" ideas or threatening them with violence looks like the will to power in operation. This coercion, however, is not Nietzschean for two reasons. First, it is conformity to the *group* that is enforced. Nietzsche would call them noisy animals seeking to alleviate anything that would cause discomfort to the herd. They are frightened of any individual who stands opposed to the majority. Greatness and the willingness to stand alone highlight the weakness and bland homogeneity of the herd. Second, this coercion is on behalf of the weak and oppressed. We must silence those who would offend, for offense is uncomfortable and we don't want anyone to feel bad. Let us then protect the delicate feelings of the oppressed and downtrodden. Needless to say, Nietzsche would despise such a motive as weakness and decadence.

To be consistent, the "justice" sought by the social justice warriors must be unmasked as an attempt to disguise the will to power in Puritan garb that makes it more appealing to the herd. There is no justice. There is only power. So too with democracy, which is another false god of a decadent, egalitarian age. While democracy promises freedom to all, Nietzsche argued that the ability to do as one pleases is predicated on one's power. Thus, freedom is the prerogative only of the very few (BGE, 29). These few are the individuals and races who exhibit lion-like qualities—Nietzsche's "blond beasts" and "master races." They are individuals powerful enough to assert dominance over others, and they are races of people powerful enough to dominate other races. Nietzsche admired Napoleon, who personified this noble ideal, (GM, I, 16) and he singled out various peoples who had done the same: "Roman, Arabian, Germanic, Japanese nobility, the Homeric heroes, the Scandinavian Viking" (GM, I, 11). It is the weak who resort to democratic institutions and churches. The strong have no interest in sharing their power or helping the widows and orphans. The weak congregate; the strong dominate.

Few have the courage or stomach for this. Even Nietzsche, for all his bravado, sometimes seemed to blink. Like the modern denizens of the radical left, Nietzsche ultimately could not extricate himself from the shadow of Christianity. He railed against it, but he could not attain a post-Christian stability. He could never relax like a satisfied atheist. Instead, he struggled against God, almost as if he secretly suspected that God existed but desperately wanted him not to, or as if he was angry that God had died. To be sure, Nietzsche argued that atheism represents the new dawn of hope for the West, which was previously trapped in the theistic cul-de-sac. But although this new atheism is obviously anti-Christian, it is not necessarily anti-religious (BGE, 54). The longings that Christianity sought to satisfy did not cease with the death of God. Atheism, Nietzsche argued, can provide the satisfaction that Christianity never could. As he put it, the "victory of atheism might free mankind of this whole feeling of guilty indebtedness.... Atheism and a kind of second innocence belong together" (GM, II, 20). Atheism holds out the promise of a new innocence, not by paying the price of guilt as Christ does but by denying the reality of guilt itself. This second innocence is a sort of return to Eden without the need for submission to a superior power or accepting an unmerited gift, both of which emphasize one's weakness and therefore one's unhappiness.

Nevertheless, Nietzsche could not help reverting to Christian categories and even Christian hopes. In a sort of ecstatic outburst, Nietzsche looked forward to the coming of a "redeeming man of great love and contempt" who will one day "bring home the *redemption* of this reality: redemption from the curse that the hitherto reigning ideal has laid upon it." This new man of the future "will redeem us not only from the hitherto reigning ideal but also from that which was bound to grow out of it, the great nausea, the will to nothingness, nihilism.... [T]his Antichrist and antinihilist; this victor over God and nothingness—*he must come one day*" (GM, II, 24).

Nietzsche did not purport to be this redeeming man of great love and contempt but saw himself, instead, as his herald— a new John the Baptist, announcing the coming of a redeemer better suited to the task than Christ, who extolled the humble and the meek, healed the sick, comforted the suffering, and saved the lost. In the place of the failed aspirations of Christianity would come a new man "whose compelling strength" would not allow him to dream of false worlds beyond our own. He would save the world from the curse of theism, which has brought with it, in its Christian manifestation, only decay, decadence, a perverse celebration of weakness, and ultimately a longing for heaven.

This longing for salvation is something Nietzsche could never shake. Obviously, if there is no God, there is no heaven, and there is no use in locating salvation in eternity or in the resurrection. Once we break free from the constraints of theism, once we recognize that salvation is conceivable only as temporal and earthbound, and once we grasp that life is nothing more than the will to power, we may be able to make the next move by simply asserting our will. The object of that assertion is not important. All that matters is willing itself. By exercising one's will, "the will itself was saved." (GM, III, 28) What one wills is not important. What matters is that one wills something. Salvation comes through an act of will.

If we are unwilling to go full Nietzsche and if Nietzschean Puritanism is riddled with incoherencies, then perhaps another path must be found. Of all the alternatives, a return to historical Christianity would be the most radical in the strict sense of the word, which is going to the root (*radix*) of the matter. Christianity, however, opens up both possibilities and problems. If God exists, then goodness, truth, and beauty have a meaning in reality that is impossible if God is dead. Likewise, the ideals of equality, democracy, tolerance, and rights make sense within Christian theism but are difficult to justify apart from it. In a Christian society, reformers can speak intelligibly about those ideals, whereas there is no justification for them if God is dead. But if God exists, and if he is the source and standard of goodness, truth, and beauty, then the will to power is not the meaning of life. Appeals to the will to power, which is divorced from the moral order of reality, get you nowhere.

Nietzschean Puritanism is incoherent, full Nietzscheanism is unlivable, and Christianity requires submission to a will greater than our own and to moral standards we did not establish. None comes without a price. In the first you must abandon reason and any hope for success; in the second you must abandon reason along with truth, goodness, and beauty; and in the third you must, as Christ put it, abandon yourself and follow him.

In Search of a Saving Myth

We began by asking what unifies our society. This is a vital question to which we must return. What binds our nation together? Are we fellow citizens or suspicious strangers? More fundamentally, can democracy survive in a world of Nietzschean Puritans? As we have seen, the answer is unambiguously no. The will to power, when unleashed, infects everything. Liberal democracy becomes a caricature of itself justifying the oppression of others in the name of abstractions such as equality, justice, and tolerance.

Centuries ago, Plato argued that democracy is fundamentally unstable and will slide toward tyranny. He believed that democratic citizens tend to deny the reality of any good beyond their appetites and any truth beyond their desires. So he proposed a "saving myth" that would reorient citizens to a moral reality above their individual desires and provide a standard of justice by which citizens could live and be governed. Nietzsche called Christianity "Platonism for the masses" because it too affirms a transcendent moral reality. Christianity provides a myth—believers would call it a true myth—that can save human beings from descending into moral nihilism and political tyranny.

Nietzsche, like Plato, recognized the indispensable power of myth:

> Without myth every culture loses the healthy natural power of its creativity: only a horizon defined by myths completes and unifies a whole cultural movement.... Images of the myth have to be the unnoticed omnipresent demonic guardians, under whose care the young soul grows to maturity and whose signs help the man to interpret his life and struggles. Even the state knows no more powerful unwritten laws than the mythical foundation that guarantees its connection with religion and its growth from mythical notions (BT, 23).

In a memorable parable, Nietzsche's alter ego, Zarathustra, descends from his mountain cave to preach a new myth: God is dead. He seeks to replace the decadent old myth with a new one characterized by the will to power (Z, Prologue). The nihilism of Nietzsche does not aim at pure destruction but at destruction for the sake of creating something new. As he put it, "If a temple is to be erected a temple must be destroyed: that is the law" (GM, II, 24).

Yet the death of God is not accomplished without a certain dread that calls for a new myth to replace the old. In another parable, Nietzsche's "madman" recognizes the problem. After bursting into the marketplace and declaring that God is dead, he grows reflective: "What water is there to clean ourselves? What festivals of atonement, what sacred games shall we have to invent?" (GS, 125). In short, what new myths will we need to create to replace the old myth we have shattered?

Nietzsche realized better than most that this new myth, like all myths, has a religious core that provides an orienting story for humanity. And even though the prospect of losing a long-established myth is disconcerting and perhaps even terrifying, Nietzsche saw what release from the moral constraints of theism made possible. Indeed, for "philosophers" and "free spirits"—those who can tolerate the loss—there is a "new dawn," a blank canvas upon which the strong and creative may exercise their freedom (GS, 343). This liberation from the strictures of the past and its badly worn theism is symbolized in the "sacred 'Yes'" uttered, as Nietzsche put it, by a child who emerges only after a lion vanquishes the fierce dragon of values, allowing the old myths to be replaced by new and more adequate ones (Z, pp. 25–27). Yet for all his celebration of this new beginning, as we have seen, there is a dark side to his vision, marked by cruelty and domination that leave most of us uncomfortable and perhaps even appalled.

Nietzsche was right. A people requires a common myth. Without a binding story shared by citizens, a nation is little more than a collection of individuals struggling to attain as much wealth, security, and power as possible. America's loss of a common myth has left us fractured and alienated, forming tribes based on interest or grievance to alleviate the loneliness.

As our society becomes more fragmented, the practice of politics as an ongoing debate about the best means to secure ends that are generally agreed upon becomes more and more difficult, while warring factions seek power above all else. True politics requires a common culture with a common set of assumptions about human nature and the social order. An ever-expanding pluralism—taken as an obvious good in our age—calls forth only a politics of power, which is in reality anti-political, for it shuns debate and abhors compromise.

Americans today embrace a variety of often competing myths, and this lack of commonality is the source of our divisions. On the one hand, our Puritan heritage has bestowed upon us certain formative stories and concepts that remain with us even though the Puritans have long since passed off the stage. For example, the Puritans referred to themselves as the "new Israel" and saw their enterprise in the New World as a latter-day Exodus: flight from oppression across a seemingly boundless wilderness to a promised land flowing with "milk and honey." The American Revolution was frequently framed as liberation from a tyrant—sometimes explicitly referred to as "Pharaoh." The civil rights movement employed similar themes of liberation from injustice. The biblical narrative of liberation is deeply embedded in the American consciousness.

From this Puritan past we have inherited a devotion to equality and justice, which we can achieve, it is thought, through social and political action. When social justice warriors demand equality or justice, they are invoking the Puritan myth, which they explicitly deny but upon which they necessarily depend. When they demand liberation of the oppressed, they are echoing the Old Testament prophets, mediated through Christianity, without which liberation gains little purchase.

At the same time, as we have seen, Nietzsche's atheistic myth has made substantial, if only partial, inroads into our consciousness. Social justice warriors embrace the tactics and rhetoric of the will to power but are unwilling fully to embrace the moral nihilism at the heart of Nietzsche's thought.

Ultimately, moral nihilism may be simply unlivable. On January 3, 1889, as Nietzsche left his apartment in Turin, he witnessed a carriage driver beating his horse. Overcome with pity, a weeping Nietzsche flung his arms around the horse to shield it from the blows. He then collapsed in the street, never recovering physically or mentally before his death in 1900. He was bedridden much of the time, his once acute and creative mind confined to rare moments of lucidity and otherwise

reduced to a confused stupor mixed with bouts of delusion—
he once referred to himself as the successor of the dead god.[1]
He occasionally composed letters, but they were the ravings
of a man far gone. The day after his collapse in the street, he
dashed off a sentence to his friend Peter Gast:

> To my maëstro Pietro.
> Sing me a new song: the world is transfigured
> and all the heavens are full of joy.
> The Crucified[2]

The man who had spent a lifetime pitting himself against
Christ came, in his insanity, to identify himself with the crucified God. Fittingly enough, Nietzsche put one of his most
vivid declarations of the death of God on the lips of a character he called the "madman." In an instance of life imitating
art, Nietzsche's final madness can be seen as a tragic realiza-
tion of his fundamental insight.

Nietzsche was buried beside his father in a traditional
Lutheran funeral that included church bells and a choir sing-
ing hymns. His coffin was decorated with a cross. Peter Gast
concluded the ceremony with a benediction, "Hallowed be
thy name to all future generations,"[3] a grotesque parody of the
Lord's Prayer identifying Nietzsche with the God he had
worked so hard to kill.

◆

We are a fractured people desperately in need of a unifying myth. Without such a myth the center cannot hold. Nietzsche offered one option, but it is not clear if even he was able to embrace it fully. Orthodox Christianity provides another, but the price seems high, especially to those who have dabbled with Nietzsche's ideas and at the same time fancy themselves men and women of a new age who pursue with self-righteous ardor the ideals of democracy, equality, social justice, and tolerance. At the very least, it is time to recognize that the merger of Nietzsche's thought with moral absolutism is doomed to intellectual incoherence and must be a source of perpetual frustration and social unrest. Perhaps the only choice really is as stark as this: Nietzsche or Christ, Dionysus or the Crucified, the will to power or the will to truth. That's how Nietzsche saw it. A bracing simplification, to be sure.

Acknowledgments

This book began to take shape when my former teacher Joshua Mitchell suggested I consult Nietzsche if I wanted to understand the social justice movement and the identity politics at its heart. I am grateful for that suggestion. Ted McAllister provided insightful feedback, especially in relation to the Puritans. Ethan Foster provided numerous comments on an early draft. I am also grateful to Les Sillars and Annabelle Mitchell for their comments. Rod Dreher was instrumental in helping this book find a home at Regnery, where Tom Spence and the rest of the folks there have been a pleasure to work with. My thanks to all.

Notes

Introduction: Nietzsche's Puritan Warriors

1. Benjamin Fearnow, "Maxine Waters: 'No Peace, No Sleep' for Trump Cabinet Members, Applauds Public Shaming," *Newsweek*, June 24, 2018, https://www.newsweek.com/maxine-waters-trump-harass-kirstjen-nielsen-stephen-miller-sarah-huckabee-993173.

2. Alexis Grenell, "White Women, Come Get Your People," *New York Times*, October 6, 2018, https://www.nytimes.com/2018/10/06/opinion/lisa-murkowski-susan-collins-kavanaugh.html.

3. Alexis de Tocqueville, *Democracy in America*, trans. Harvey C. Mansfield and Delba Winthrop (Chicago: University of Chicago Press, 2000), 28.

4. Rüdiger Safranski, *Nietzsche: A Philosophical Biography*, trans. Shelley Frisch (New York: Norton, 2003), 351.

5. Ibid., 352.

6. Ibid., 353.

7. Ronald Hayman, *Nietzsche: A Critical Life* (New York: Penguin Books, 1982), 64.

8. Ibid., 66.

9. Walter Kaufmann, ed., *The Portable Nietzsche*, (New York: Penguin, 1976), 103–4.

10. Safranski, *Nietzsche: A Philosophical Biography*, 356.

11. Ibid., 367.

12. Ibid., 315.

13. Ibid., 20.

Chapter 1: *My Truth, Your Truth, God and Values*

1. I realize some readers will accuse me of ignoring the distinction between sex and gender and that my argument fails if sex and gender are separable. Quite true, but this is precisely what I am denying. One does not choose one's sex. And sex and gender are, ultimately, inseparable.

2. A brief one can be found in Paul C. Vitz, *Faith of the Fatherless: The Psychology of Atheism* (San Francisco: Ignatius Press, 2013, originally published in 1999).

Chapter 2: *Protest Trumps Debate*

1. Scott Jaschik, "Shouting Down a Lecture," Inside Higher Ed, March 3, 2017, https://www.insidehighered.com/news/2017/03/03/middlebury-students-shout-down-lecture-charles-murray.

2. "Google's Ideological Echo Chamber," Wikipedia, https://en.wikipedia.org/wiki/Google%27s_Ideological_Echo_Chamber.

3. Rasmussen Reports, "31% Think U.S. Civil War Likely Soon," June 27, 2018, http://www.rasmussenreports.com/public_content/politics/general_politics/june_2018/31_think_u_s_civil_war_likely_soon.

4. The American "Revolution" is misnamed, for while the colonists threw out the British and established their own government, they had no intention of remaking their society according to some perfectionist vision. As Russell Kirk insists, it was a revolution not made but prevented. Americans at the time tended to be deeply skeptical of utopian aspirations. They were sober enough—Augustinian enough, even if the Christian commitments of some were wavering—not to be taken in by promises of social perfection.

Chapter 3: Democracy as Decadence

1. It is important to note that though democracy was born in ancient Greece, *modern* democracy emerged much later. In Greek democracy, citizenship was restricted to a relatively small class of men, whereas modern democracy is characterized by an expanding view of citizenship in keeping with the notion of universal dignity, rights, and equality.

Chapter 5: Memory, Monuments, and Manipulation

1. "ALA, ALSC Respond to Wilder Medal Name Change," American Library Association, June 25, 2018, http://www.ala.org/news/press-releases/2018/06/ala-alsc-respond-wilder-medal-name-change.
2. Rozina Sabur, "Harper Lee and Mark Twain Banned by Minnesota Schools Over Racial Slurs," *Telegraph*, February 12, 2018, https://www.telegraph.co.uk/news/2018/02/12/harper-lee-mark-twain-banned-minnesota-schools/.
3. Zachery Eanes, "Durham Confederate Statue: Tribute to Dying Veterans or Political Tool of Jim Crow South?" *News & Observer*, August 16, 2017, https://www.newsobserver.com/news/local/counties/durham-county/article167672037.html.

4. Emily Ferguson, "Pepperdine Will Remove Christopher Columbus Statue," Washington Free Beacon, February 2, 2017, http://freebeacon.com/culture/pepperdine-will-remove-christopher-columbus-statue/.

Chapter 6: OMG! The Weaponization of Language
1. Saul Alinsky, *Rules for Radicals* (New York: Vintage Books, 1989), 3.
2. Ibid., 10.
3. Ibid., 4.
4. Ibid., 36.

Chapter 7: Life, Death, Sex, Babies, and Gender
1. Peter Singer, "Heavy Petting," Utilitarian.net, 2001, https://www.utilitarian.net/singer/by/2001----.htm.

Chapter 8: Creating the Overman: Technology and the Promise of Unlimited Power
1. Richard Freed, "The Tech Industry's War on Kids," Medium, March 12, 2018, https://medium.com/@richardnfreed/the-tech-industrys-psychological-war-on-kids-c452870464ce.
2. See Transcendent Man, https://transcendentman.com/.
3. "Sprint I Am Unlimited Ad," YouTube, January 31, 2013, https://www.youtube.com/watch?v=GCUO3-yq3eg.

Conclusion: In Search of a Saving Myth
1. Ronald Hayman, *Nietzsche: A Critical Life* (New York: Penguin Books, 1982), 336.
2. Walter Kaufmann, ed., *The Portable Nietzsche*, (New York: Penguin, 1976), 685.
3. Hayman, 350.

Index

A

Abolition of Man, The, 101
abortion, 91–93
African Americans, 68
Alinsky, Saul, 33, 81
Amazon, 95
American Dream, 6
American Library Association (ALA), 67–68
American Revolution, 135
Antifa, 34
Aristotle, 23, 71, 84
Augustine, 37, 63

B

Bacon, Francis, 96–97, 108–9
Big Brother, 79–80
Big Tech, 95
Bondi, Pam, 32
brain-hacking, 95

C

Christianity, 8, 24–25, 27, 29–30, 40, 43, 51–52, 54–57, 60, 62–63, 66–67, 99–100, 113, 116–17, 119–23, 127–30, 132, 135, 137
City of God, 37, 63
City of God, The, 63

civil society, 6
Civil War monuments, 69
classical education, 110–11
Collins, Susan, 4
Columbus, Christopher, 69
common good, 5, 22, 34–36
consent, 45–46, 87
created order, 74, 76, 78, 86, 120

D

Damore, James, 32
death of God, 21–22, 27, 30, 37, 52, 128, 133, 136
death with dignity, 94
democracy, 8, 37, 41–44, 46, 77, 115, 117, 121, 127, 130–31, 137
Dionysus, 30, 137
diversity, 10, 82, 115
divine command, 120
divine redemption, 9
Dolezal, Rachel, 21

E

Earthly City, 37–38
egalitarianism, 120
evil, 3, 10, 13, 16–17, 22, 26, 28, 37, 42, 76, 85, 98, 112, 116, 120, 122

F

Facebook, 43, 95
Fair, Christine, 2
Flake, Jeff, 2
forgiveness, 29, 56–57, 59–60, 123
French Revolution, 38

G

gender fluidity, 85
gender traitors, 3
Golden Rule, 22, 44, 88
Google, 32, 95, 97
Gospel of John, 74
Gospel of Matthew, 57
Grenell, Alexis, 3–4

H

Hawthorne, Nathaniel, 9
Heraclitus of Ephesus, 24
higher education, 107, 110, 112–14
Hobbes, Thomas, 45, 76
Huckleberry Finn, 68–69
human nature, 35–36, 59, 76, 84–86, 91, 93, 134

I

identity politics, 11, 49, 54, 56–57, 60–61, 69, 117, 123, 139
imago Dei, 72–73, 124
individual rights, 115
instinct, 52, 62, 76, 86–87, 120
iPhone, 95–96

K

Kantians, 27
Kavanaugh, Brett, 2–4

L

last man, the, 43, 98
Laura Ingalls Wilder Medal, 67
left-wing radicals, 34
legitimate power, 120
Lewis, C. S., 101
LGBT+ movement, 90
liberalism, 47–48
Locke, John, 45
logic of history, 11
logos, 24, 74–75, 77

M

Mann, Thomas, 13
marriage, 18, 85–86
metaphysical skepticism, 122
Middlebury College, 31
moral absolutism, 37, 68, 91, 113, 120–21, 137
moral epoch, the, 52
moral nihilism, 132, 135
moral relativism, 35, 69
moral terms, 28, 55, 77
moral truths, 19
Murray, Charles, 31

N

Native Americans, 68
natural law, 22
New Deal, 6
New Testament, 41

new world, 26, 91, 105, 115, 134
Newspeak, 79
Nielsen, Kirstjen, 32
Nietzschean psychology, 58
Nietzschean Puritanism, 104, 130
Nietzschean will to power, 9, 35, 92, 119–20
Nineteen Eighty-Four, 79

O
Obama, Barack, 33, 81
objective truth, 112
Old Testament, 41–42, 135
On the Future of Our Educational Institutions, 108
original sin, 9
orthodoxy, 10–11, 31, 120
Orwell, George, 79
Overman, the (*Übermensch*), 17, 95, 98–99

P
paganism, 51, 66
patriarchy, 4, 6–7, 56, 113, 117, 121
Pelosi, Nancy, 33
philology, 13
Plato, 23–24, 46, 63, 72, 75–76, 131–32
Platonism, 24, 132
Plymouth colony, 50
political perfection, 38
political tyranny, 132
pornography, 89–90

procreation, 85
progressivism, 6, 9
prostitution, 89
Puritanism, 8, 37, 104, 123, 130

R
radical left, 9, 11, 37, 119–20, 127
radicalism, 5
Rasmussen Report, 34
rational speech, 71, 81
Rousseau, Jean-Jacques, 45
Rules for Radicals, 33, 81

S
safe spaces, 107, 113–14
Saint John, 24
salvation, 29–30, 129–30
Sanders, Sarah Huckabee, 33
scapegoating, 49, 54
Schumer, Charles, 33
scientific elite, 96–97
self-government, 111–12
self-sacrifice, 52
sexual assault, 3
Shields, Annie, 2
Singer, Peter, 87–88
slavery, 6, 48, 50
social contract, 46
social justice warriors, 9, 11, 35, 37, 80, 121–24, 126–27, 135
Sophists, 75
Sprint, 102–4

T
technology, 95–97, 99, 101, 103, 105
teleological view of history, 61, 64
theism, 25, 78, 100, 129–30, 133
To Kill a Mockingbird, 68
Tocqueville, Alexis de, 7, 46
tolerance, 31, 37, 67–68, 82, 113–15, 118, 121–22, 126, 130–31, 137
transhumanists, 98–99
transvaluation of values, 28, 30
trigger warnings, 114

U
U.S. Supreme Court, 2–3
University of Basel, 14
University of Bonn, 13
Unmoved Mover, 84
utilitarians, 27

V
vice, 9, 20, 55, 69
virtue, 9, 43, 45, 55–56, 68, 70, 75, 83, 92, 124

W
war rhetoric, 40
Waters, Maxine, 1, 33
Western culture, 21, 125
white nationalists, 33–34
white privilege, 56

will to power, 7, 9, 12, 16, 25, 27–28, 30, 35–37, 42, 44–46, 51–54, 57, 59, 62, 64, 74–75, 77–78, 85–87, 89–94, 100–101, 105, 109, 113–17, 119–21, 124, 126–27, 129–32, 135, 137
World War I, 6

Z
Zarathustra, 102, 132